FRENCH

in 10 minutes a day®

by **Kristine Kershul**, M.A., University of California, Santa Barbara

adapted by **Jan Fisher Brousseau**

W9-AYG-503

A Sunset Series — Sunset Publishing Corporation
Menlo Park, California

Fourth printing August 1991

L'alphabet

Many French letters sound the same as in English, but some French letters are pronounced or written differently. To learn the French sounds of these letters, write each example in the space provided in addition to saying the word many times. After you practice the word see if you can locate it on the map.

French letter	English sound	Example	(Write it here)
a	ah	Paris (pah-ree)	
au/eau	oh/oe	Bordeaux (bore-doe)	
c (before, a,o,u)	k	Carcassonne (kar-kah-sohn)	
c (before e,i,y)	s	Nice (nees)	Nice
ç	s	Alençon (ah-lah$^{(n)}$-soh$^{(n)}$)	
ch	sh	Champagne (shah$^{(n)}$-pahn-yuh)	
e	uh	Le Mans (luh mah$^{(n)}$)	
é	ay	Orléans (or-lay-ah$^{(n)}$)	
ei	eh	Seine (sehn)	
è/ê	e (as in let)	Norvège (nor-vezh)	
g (before a,o,u)	g	Garonne (gar-own)	
g (before e,i,y)	zh (as in leisure)	Gironde (zhee-rohnd)	
gn	ny (as in onion)	Avignon (ah-veen-yoh$^{(n)}$)	
i	ee	Lille (leel)	
j	zh	Le Jura (luh zhew-rah)	
o	oh	Limoges (lee-mohzh)	
qu	k	Québec (kay-bek)	
r	(slightly rolled)	Rennes (ren)	
s (between vowels)	z	Toulouse (too-looz)	
u	ew/ue	Tunisie (tew-nee-zee)	
x (varies)	gz	Exeter (eg-zuh-tare)	
	ks	Luxembourg (lewk-sum-boor)	
	s	Auxerre (oh-sair)	Auxerre
y	ee	Nancy (nah$^{(n)}$-see)	

NASAL VOWEL SOUNDS

am, an, em, en	ah$^{(n)}$ (taunt nasalized)	Angleterre (ah$^{(n)}$-gluh-tare)	
im, in, aim, ain, ein, eim	a$^{(n)}$ (than nasalized)	Reims (ra$^{(n)}$s)	
om, on	oh$^{(n)}$ (don't nasalized)	Toulon (too-loh$^{(n)}$)	
um, un	uh$^{(n)}$ (fun nasalized)	Melun (mel-uh$^{(n)}$)	

Seven Key Question Words

Step 1

When you arrive in **France** *(frah⁽ⁿ⁾-s)* or **Québec,** *(kay-bek)* the very first thing you will need to do is to ask

questions — "Where is the train station?" "Where can I exchange money?" "Where

(où) *(oo)* is the lavatory?" **"Où** is the restaurant?" **"Où** do I catch a taxi?" **"Où** is

a good hotel?" **"Où** is my luggage?" — and the list will go on and on for the entire length

of your visit. In French, there are SEVEN KEY QUESTION WORDS to learn. For

example, the seven key question words will help you to find out exactly what you are

ordering in a restaurant before you order it — and not after the surprise (or shock!) arrives.

Take a few minutes to study and practice saying the seven basic question words listed

below. Notice that "what" and "who" are only differentiated by one letter, so be sure not

to confuse them. Then cover the French words with your hand and fill in each of the

blanks with the matching **mot français.** *(mow)* *(frah⁽ⁿ⁾-say)* word French

1.	**OÙ** *(oo)*	=	WHERE	*où, où, où, où, où*
2.	**QUI** *(key)*	=	WHO	_____
3.	**QUE/QU'** *(kuh)*	=	WHAT	_____
4.	**POURQUOI** *(poor-kwah)*	=	WHY	_____
5.	**QUAND** *(kah⁽ⁿ⁾)*	=	WHEN	_____
6.	**COMMENT** *(ko-mah⁽ⁿ⁾)*	=	HOW	_____
7.	**COMBIEN** *(kohm-bee-yen)*	=	HOW MUCH	_____

3

Now test yourself to see if you really can keep these **mots** ^(mow) straight in your mind. Draw lines between the French **et** ^(ay) English equivalents below.

why   **qui**

what   **que**

who   **où**

how   **combien**

where   **quand**

when   **pourquoi**

how much   **comment**

Examine the following questions containing these **mots.** ^(mow) Practice the sentences out loud many times **et** ^(ay) then quiz yourself by filling in the blanks below with the correct question **mot.**

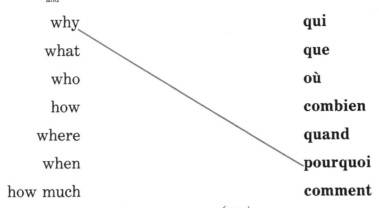

Où est le téléphone? ^{(oo) (ay) (luh) (tay-lay-phone)}
Where is the telephone?

Qui est-ce? ^{(key) (ess)}
Who is it?

Combien est-ce? ^{(kohm-bee-yen) (ess)}
How much is it?

Quand le train arrive-t-il? ^{(kah(n)) (luh) (tra(n)) (ah-reev-teel)}
When the train does it arrive?

Qu'est-ce qui se passe? ^{(kess) (key) (suh) (pahss)}
What's happening?

Comment est la salade? ^{(ko-mah(n)) (ay) (lah) (sah-lahd)}
How is the salad?

Qu'est-ce que c'est? ^{(kess) (kuh) (say)}
What is it?

Pourquoi le train n'arrive-t-il pas? ^{(poor-kwah) (luh)(tra(n)) (nah-reev-teel) (pah)}
Why doesn't it arrive?

1. _Comment_ est la salade?

2. _____ est-ce?

3. _____ est-ce qui se passe?

4. _____ est le téléphone?

5. _____ le train n'arrive-t-il pas?

6. _____ est-ce?

7. _____ le train arrive-t-il?

8. _____ est-ce que c'est?

Où will be your most used question **mot,** so let's concentrate on it. **Répétez** ^(ray-pay-tay) the repeat following French sentences aloud. Then write out each sentence without looking at the **exemple.** ^(eg-zahm-pluh) If you don't succeed on the first try, don't give up. Just practice each sentence until you are able to do it easily. Don't forget that **"qu"** is pronounced like "k" and

"est-ce" like "ess." Also, in French, the letter **"h"** is silent and **"th"** is pronounced like "t."

(soh⁽ⁿ⁾) — **Où sont** *(lay) (kah-bee-nay)* **les cabinets?** / *(twah-let)* **les toilettes?**

 messieurs dames

(ay) (luh) (tahx-ee)
Où est le taxi?

(ay) (low-toe-boos)
Où est l'autobus?

_____   *Où est le taxi?*   _____

(ay) (luh) (res-toe-rah⁽ⁿ⁾)
Où est le restaurant?

(lah) (bah⁽ⁿ⁾k)
Où est la banque?

(low-tell)
Où est l'hôtel?

_____   _____   _____

(wee)
Oui, many of the **mots** which look like **anglais** are also **français.** Since **français et**
yes ... *(mow)* mots ... *(ah⁽ⁿ⁾-glay)* English anglais ... *(frah⁽ⁿ⁾-say)* French français ... *(ay)* et

anglais share many words, your work here **est** simpler. You will be amazed at the
(ay) is

number of **mots** which are **identiques** (or almost **identiques**). Of course, they do not
(ee-dah⁽ⁿ⁾-teak) identical

always sound the same when spoken by a French person, but the **similarité** will
(see-mee-lar-ee-tay) similarity

certainly surprise you. Listed below are five "free" **mots** beginning with "A" to

help you get started. Be sure to say each **mot** aloud **et** then write out the **mot français**
(ay) et ... *(frah⁽ⁿ⁾-say)*

in the blank to the right.

☑ **l'accident** *(lack-see-dah⁽ⁿ⁾)* . . . . accident _____
☑ **l'addition** *(lah-dee-see-oh⁽ⁿ⁾)* . . . . the bill in a restaurant _____
☑ **l'admission** *(lahd-mee-see-oh⁽ⁿ⁾)* . . . . admission _____
☑ **l'adresse** *(lah-dress)* . . . . address *l'adresse*
☑ **aidez-moi!** *(ay-day-mwah)* . . . . aid me! help me! _____

Free **mots** like these will appear at the bottom of the following pages in a yellow color

band. They are easy — enjoy them!

Step 2

"the," "a," "some"

All of these words mean "the" in **français**:

(luh) **le**	*(lah)* **la**	**l'**	*(lay)* **les**

(gar-soh⁽ⁿ⁾)			*(gar-soh⁽ⁿ⁾)*
le garçon:	the boy	**les garçons:**	the boys
(fee-yah) **la fille:**	the girl	*(fee-yah)* **les filles:**	the girls
(lome) **l'homme:**	the man	*(lay-zome)* **les hommes:**	the men

These two words mean "a" or "an":

(uh⁽ⁿ⁾) **un**	*(ewn)* **une**

These words mean "some":

(dew) **du**	*(duh lah)* **de la**	*(duh)* **de l'**	*(day)* **des**

(tra⁽ⁿ⁾) **un train:**	a train
(uh-nome) **un homme:**	a man
(fahm) **une femme:**	a woman
(sah-lahd) **une salade:**	a salad

(soo-kruh) **du sucre:**	some sugar
(moo-tard) **de la moutarde:**	some mustard
(la⁽ⁿ⁾-tay-ray) **de l'intérêt:**	some interest
(fwee) **des fruits:**	some fruits

Le français *(frah⁽ⁿ⁾-say)* / French — has multiple **mots** for "the," "a" and "some," but there **est** *(ay)* / is — no need to worry about it. Just make a choice **et** *(ay)* remember to use one of these **mots** when you mean "the," "a" **ou** *(oo)* / or — "some."

Step 3

Les Choses
(lay) *(showz)* — things

Before you proceed **avec** *(ah-vek)* / with — this step, situate yourself comfortably in your living room. Now look around you. Can you name the things which you see in this **pièce** *(pea-ess)* / room — in **français?** Probably you can guess **la lampe** *(lahmp)* and maybe even **la chaise.** *(shehz)* Let's learn the rest of them.

After practicing these **mots** out loud, write them in the blanks below **et** *(ay)* on the next page.

(tah-blow) **le tableau**	= the picture	*le tableau*
(plah-foh⁽ⁿ⁾) **le plafond**	= the ceiling	_____

☑ **l'alcool** *(lahl-kohl)* . . . . alcohol _____
☐ **les Alpes** *(lay zahlp)* . . . . the Alps _____
☐ **américain** *(ah-may-ree-ka⁽ⁿ⁾)* . . . . American _____
☐ **l'animal** *(lah-nee-mawl)* . . . . animal _____
6 ☐ **l'appartement** *(lah-par-teh-mah⁽ⁿ⁾)* . . . . . apartment _____

(kwa(n)) **le coin**	= the corner _____	
(fuh-net-ruh) **la fenêtre**	= the window _____	
(lahmp) **la lampe**	= the lamp _____	
(lew-mee-air) **la lumière**	= the light _____	
(kah-nah-pay) **le canapé**	= the sofa _____	
(shehz) **la chaise**	= the chair _____	
(tah-pee) **le tapis**	= the carpet _____	
(tahb-luh) **la table**	= the table *la table*	
(port) **la porte**	= the door _____	
(pah(n)-dewl) **la pendule**	= the clock _____	
(ree-doe) **le rideau**	= the curtain _____	
(mewr) **le mur**	= the wall _____	

You will notice that the correct form of **le, la ou les** is given *(oo)* **avec** *(ah-vek)* each noun. This is for your
with

information — just remember to use one of them. Now open your book to the first page

avec the stick-on labels. Peel off the first 14 labels **et** *(ay)* proceed around the **pièce,** *(pea-ess)*
room

labeling these items in your home. This will help to increase your French **mot** power easily.

Don't forget to say **le mot** as you attach each label.

Now ask yourself, **"Où est le tableau?"** *(luh) (tah-blow)* **et** point at it while you answer, **"Voilà** *(vwah-lah)*
there is

le tableau." Continue on down the **liste** *(least)* until you feel comfortable with these new
list

mots. Say, **"Où est le plafond?"** *(plah-foh(n))* Then **répondez,** *(ray-poh(n)-day)* **"Voilà le plafond,"** *(luh)* and so on.
respond

When you can identify all the items on the **liste,** *(least)* you will be ready to move on.

Now, starting on the next page, let's learn some basic parts of the house.

☐ **l'appétit** *(lah-pay-tee)*	appetite	_____
☐ **l'arrêt** *(lah-ray)*	stop, arrest	_____
☐ **l'arrivée** *(lah-ree-vay)*	arrival	_____
☐ **l'attention** *(lah-tah(n)-see-oh(n))*	attention	_____
☐ **l'auteur** *(low-tur)*	author	_____

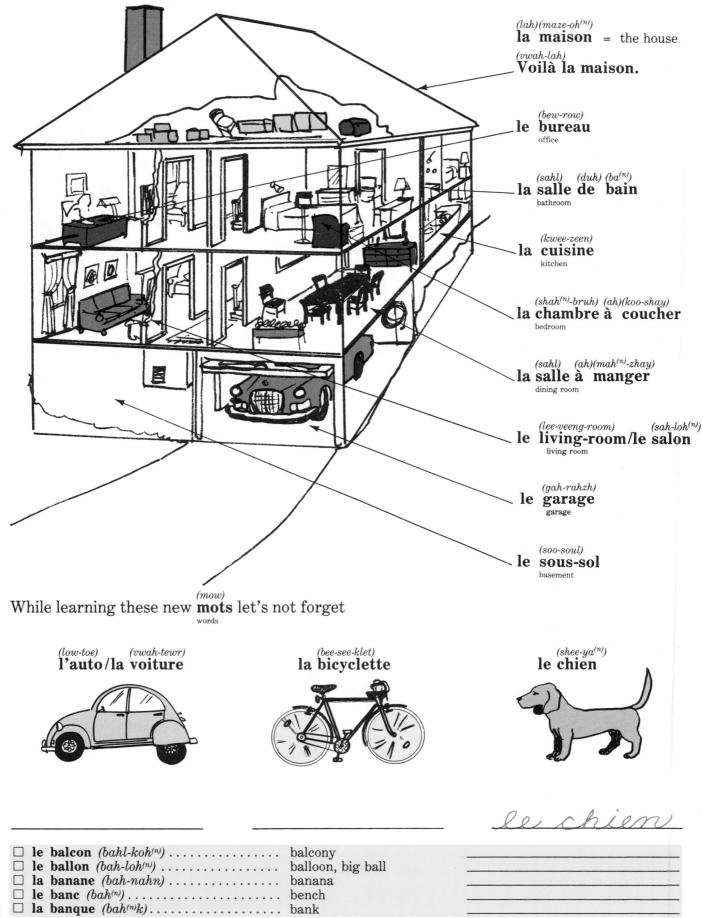

(lah)(maze-oh⁽ⁿ⁾)
la maison = the house

(vwah-lah)
Voilà la maison.

(bew-row)
le bureau
office

(sahl) (duh) (ba⁽ⁿ⁾)
la salle de bain
bathroom

(kwee-zeen)
la cuisine
kitchen

(shah⁽ⁿ⁾-bruh) (ah)(koo-shay)
la chambre à coucher
bedroom

(sahl) (ah)(mah⁽ⁿ⁾-zhay)
la salle à manger
dining room

(lee-veeng-room) (sah-loh⁽ⁿ⁾)
le living-room/le salon
living room

(gah-rahzh)
le garage
garage

(soo-soul)
le sous-sol
basement

(mow)
While learning these new **mots** let's not forget
words

(low-toe) *(vwah-tewr)*
l'auto/la voiture

(bee-see-klet)
la bicyclette

(shee-ya⁽ⁿ⁾)
le chien

le chien

☐ **le balcon** *(bahl-koh⁽ⁿ⁾)*	balcony
☐ **le ballon** *(bah-loh⁽ⁿ⁾)*	balloon, big ball
☐ **la banane** *(bah-nahn)*	banana
☐ **le banc** *(bah⁽ⁿ⁾)*	bench
☐ **la banque** *(bah⁽ⁿ⁾k)*	bank

(shah)
le chat
cat

(zhar-da$^{(n)}$)
le jardin
garden

(koo-ree-ay)
le courrier
mail

le jardin

(bwaht) (oh) (let-ruh)
la boîte aux lettres
mail box

(fluhr)
les fleurs
flowers

(so-net)
la sonnette
door bell

Peel off the next set of labels *(ay)* **et** wander through your **maison** *(maze-oh$^{(n)}$)* learning these new **mots.** *(mow)*

Granted, it will be somewhat difficult to label your **chien, chat ou fleurs,** but use your

(ee-mah-zhee-nah-see-oh$^{(n)}$)
imagination.

Again, practice by asking yourself, **"Où est le jardin?"** et **répondez,** *(ray-poh$^{(n)}$-day)* **"Voilà le jardin."**

Où est

☐ **le bifteck** *(beef-tek)* .... beefsteak	
☐ **le biscuit** *(bee-skwee)* .... cookie	
☐ **la bouteille** *(boo-tay)* .... bottle	
☐ **bref** *(brehf)* .... brief, short	
☐ **brillant** *(bree-yah$^{(n)}$)* .... brilliant, sparkling	

Step 4

(uh⁽ⁿ⁾) *(duh)* *(twah)*
Un, deux, trois
one   two   three

(ah⁽ⁿ⁾-fah⁽ⁿ⁾) *(ray-seat)*
This is part of a little rhyme that **les enfants français récitent**:
children   recite

(uh⁽ⁿ⁾) (duh) (twah) **Un, deux, trois** one two three	*(zhuh) (vay) (dah⁽ⁿ⁾) (lay) (bwah)* **je vais dans les bois** I go into the woods
(kah-truh) (sank) (sees) **Quatre, cinq, six** four five six	*(kuh-year) (day) (sir-eez)* **cueillir des cerises.** to pick some cherries

For some reason, numbers are not the easiest thing to learn, but just remember how

(koh⁽ⁿ⁾-vair-sah-see-oh⁽ⁿ⁾)
important they are in everyday **conversation.** How could you tell someone your phone
conversation

number, your address or your hotel room if you had no numbers. And think of how

difficult it would be if you could not understand the time, the price of an apple or the

(nome-bruh) *(see-mee-lar-ee-tay)*
correct bus to take. When practicing the **nombres** below, notice the **similarités** between
numbers   similarities

(kah-truh) *(kah-torz)* *(set)* *(deez-set)*
quatre (4) and **quatorze** (14), **sept** (7) and **dix-sept** (17) **et** so on.

0	*(zay-row)* **zéro**			0 *zéro, zéro, zéro*
1	*(uh⁽ⁿ⁾)* **un**	**11**	*(oh⁽ⁿ⁾z)* **onze**	1
2	*(duh)* **deux**	**12**	*(dues)* **douze**	2
3	*(twah)* **trois**	**13**	*(trehz)* **treize**	3
4	*(kah-truh)* **quatre**	**14**	*(kah-torz)* **quatorze**	4
5	*(sank)* **cinq**	**15**	*(ka⁽ⁿ⁾z)* **quinze**	5
6	*(sees)* **six**	**16**	*(says)* **seize**	6
7	*(set)* **sept**	**17**	*(deez-set)* **dix-sept**	7
8	*(wheat)* **huit**	**18**	*(deez-wheat)* **dix-huit**	8
9	*(nuf)* **neuf**	**19**	*(deez-nuf)* **dix-neuf**	9
10	*(dees)* **dix**	**20**	*(va⁽ⁿ⁾)* **vingt**	10

☐ **la capitale** *(kah-pee-tahl)* . . . . capital
☐ **la cathédrale** *(kah-tay-drahl)* . . . . cathedral
☐ **le cendrier** *(sah⁽ⁿ⁾-dree-ay)* . . . . ashtray (cinders)
☐ **le centre** *(sah⁽ⁿ⁾-truh)* . . . . center
☐ **le champagne** *(shah⁽ⁿ⁾-pan-yuh)* . . . . champagne

(ew-tee-lee-zay) *(nome-bruh)*
Utilisez these **nombres** on a daily basis. Count to yourself **en français** *(ah⁽ⁿ⁾)* when you brush
use

your teeth, exercise, **ou** *(oo)* commute to work. Now fill in the following blanks according to
or

the **nombres** given in parentheses.

Note: This is a good time to start learning these two important phrases.

(zhuh) *(voo-dray)*
Je voudrais = I would like _____

(new) *(voo-dree-oh⁽ⁿ⁾)*
Nous voudrions = we would like _____

(zhuh) (voo-dray) **Je voudrais** _____ (15)	*(fuh-yuh) (duh) (pah-pee-ay)* **feuilles de papier.** sheets of paper	*(kohm-bee-yen)* **Combien?** _____ (15)
Je voudrais _____ (10)	*(kart) (pohs-tall)* **cartes postales.** postcards	**Combien?** _____ (10)
Je voudrais _____ (11)	*(ta⁽ⁿ⁾-bruh-post)* **timbres-poste.** stamps	**Combien?** _____ (11)
Je voudrais _____ (8)	*(lee-truh) (day-sah⁽ⁿ⁾-s)* **litres d'essence.** liters of gas	**Combien?** *huit* (8)
Je voudrais _____ (1)	*(vair) (duh) (zhew) (door-ah⁽ⁿ⁾zh)* **verre de jus d'orange.** glass of orange juice	**Combien?** _____ (1)
(new) (voo-dree-oh⁽ⁿ⁾) **Nous voudrions** _____ (3)	*(tahs) (duh) (tay)* **tasses de thé.** cups of tea	**Combien?** _____ (3)
Nous voudrions _____ (4)	*(tee-kay) (doe-toe-boos)* **tickets d'autobus.** bus tickets	**Combien?** _____ (4)
Nous voudrions *deux* (2)	*(bee-air)* **bières.** beers	**Combien?** _____ (2)
Je voudrais _____ (12)	*(uh) (fray)* **oeufs frais.** eggs fresh	**Combien?** _____ (12)
Nous voudrions _____ (6)	*(lee-vruh) (duh) (vee-ah⁽ⁿ⁾d)* **livres de viande.** pounds of meat	**Combien?** _____ (6)
Nous voudrions _____ (5)	*(vair) (doe)* **verres d'eau.** glasses of water	**Combien?** _____ (5)
Je voudrais _____ (7)	*(vair) (duh) (va⁽ⁿ⁾)* **verres de vin.** glasses of wine	**Combien?** _____ (7)
Nous voudrions _____ (9)	*(lee-vruh) (duh) (buhr)* **livres de beurre.** pounds of butter	**Combien?** _____ (9)

☐ **le changement** *(shah⁽ⁿ⁾-zhuh-mah⁽ⁿ⁾)* . . . . change _____
☐ **le chèque** *(shek)* . . . . bank check _____
☐ **le chocolat** *(show-ko-lah)* . . . . chocolate _____
☐ **le coiffeur** *(kwah-fur)* . . . . hairdresser _____
☐ **la communication** *(ko-mew-nee-kah-see-oh⁽ⁿ⁾)* . communication _____

11

Now see if you can translate the following thoughts into **français.** **Les** *(lay)* **réponses** *(ray-poh⁽ⁿ⁾s)* are at the bottom of the **page.** *(pahzh)*

1. I would like seven postcards.

_____

2. I would like one beer.

Je voudrais une bière.

3. We would like two glasses of water.

_____

4. We would like three bus tickets.

_____

Review **les nombres** 1 **à** 20 **et** answer the following **questions** *(kehs-tee-oh⁽ⁿ⁾)* aloud, **et** then write the **réponses** *(ray-poh⁽ⁿ⁾s)* in the blank spaces to the left.

Combien de tables y *(kohm-bee-yen) (duh) (tahb-luh) (ee)* are
a-t-il ici? *(ah-teel) (ee-see)* there here

trois

Combien de lampes y *(lahmp) (ee)*
a-t-il ici? *(ah-teel) (ee-see)*

_____

Combien de chaises y a-t-il ici? *(shehz)*

_____

12

Combien de pendules *(duh) (pah(n)-dewl) (ee)* **y a-t-il ici?** *(ah-teel)*

_____

Combien de fenêtres *(fuh-net-ruh)* **y a-t-il ici?**

une _____

Combien de personnes *(pear-sohn)* **y a-t-il ici?**

_____

Combien d'hommes *(dome)* **y a-t-il ici?**

_____

Combien de femmes *(fahm)* **y a-t-il ici?**

_____

| **Les Couleurs** *(lay) (koo-luhr)* colors | **Step 5** |

Les couleurs sont *(soh(n))* the same **en France et au Québec** *(ah(n))(frah(n)-s) (oh) (kay-bek)* as **en Amérique** *(ah(n))(nah-may-reek)*—they just have
are   in   in

different **noms.** *(noh(n))* You can easily recognize **violet** *(vee-oh-lay)* as violet and **bleu** *(bluh)* as blue. So when
names

you are invited to someone's **maison et** *(maze-oh(n))* you want to bring flowers, you will be able to order
house

the **couleur correcte** *(ko-rekt)* of flowers. (Contrary to American custom, **en Europe les fleurs** *(ah(n))(nuh-rope) (fluhr)*

rouges, et *(roozh)* particularly **les roses rouges,** *(rose)* are only exchanged between lovers!) Let's
red

learn the basic **couleurs.** *(koo-luhr)* Once you have read through **la liste** *(least)* on the next **page,** *(pahzh)* cover

the **français avec** your **main, et** *(ma(n))* practice writing out the **français** next to the **anglais.**
with   hand

Notice the **similarités** *(see-mee-lar-ee-tay)* between **les mots en français et en anglais.** *(ah(n))(frah(n)-say) (ah(n))(nah(n)-glay)*

☐ **la compagnie** *(koh(n)-pahn-yee)* . . . . company   _____
☐ **le/la concierge** *(koh(n)-see-airzh)* . . . . doorkeeper   _____
☐ **la conversation** *(koh(n)-vair-sah-see-oh(n))* . . . conversation   _____
☐ **le cousin** *(koo-za(n))* . . . . cousin (male)   _____
☐ **la cousine** *(koo-zeen)* . . . . cousin (female)   _____

(blah⁽ⁿ⁾)
blanc = white _____ (bah-toe) (ay)
Le bateau est blanc.
boat

(nwahr)
noir = black _____ (bawl)
La balle est noire.

(zhown)
jaune = yellow _____ (bah-nahn)
La banane est jaune.

(roozh)
rouge = red _____ (lee-vruh)
Le livre est rouge.
book

(bluh)
bleu = blue _*bleu*_ (low-toe)
L'auto est bleue.

(gree)
gris = gray _____ (lay-lay-fah⁽ⁿ⁾)
L'éléphant est gris.

(mah-roh⁽ⁿ⁾)
marron = brown _____ (shehz)
La chaise est marron.
chair

(vair)
vert = green _____ (peh-looz) (vairt)
La pelouse est verte.
grass

(rose)
rose = pink _____ (fluhr)
La fleur est rose.

(mewl-tee-ko-lor)
multicolore = multi-colored _____ (lahmp)
La lampe est multicolore.

Now peel off the next (dees) **dix** labels **et** proceed to label these **couleurs** (koo-luhr) **dans** (dah⁽ⁿ⁾) your **maison.** (maze-oh⁽ⁿ⁾)
in

Now let's practice using these **mots.**

Où est le bateau blanc?   (vwah-lah) **Voilà le bateau** _*blanc*_.
there is

Où est la table grise?   **Voilà la table** _____.

Où est la chaise marron?   **Voilà la chaise** _____.

Où est la balle blanche? (blah⁽ⁿ⁾-shuh)   **Voilà la balle** _____.

Où est la lampe multicolore?   **Voilà la lampe** _____.

Où est le livre rouge?   **Voilà le livre** _____.

☐ **la dame** (dahm) . . . . lady _____
☐ **la danse** (dah⁽ⁿ⁾-s) . . . . dance _____
☐ **décembre** (day-sah⁽ⁿ⁾m-bruh) . . . . December _____
☐ **la déclaration** (day-klah-rah-see-oh⁽ⁿ⁾) . . . declaration _____
14 ☐ **le départ** (day-par) . . . . departure _____

Où est la porte **verte**? *(vairt)*   Voilà la porte _____.

Où est la maison rose?   Voilà la maison _____.

Où est la banane jaune?   Voilà la banane _____.

Note: **En français,** *(ah⁽ⁿ⁾) (frah⁽ⁿ⁾-say)* the **verbe** for "to have" **est "avoir."** *(vairb)* *(ah-vwahr)*

(zhay)
j'ai = I have_____   **nous avons** = we have_____ *(new) (zah-voh⁽ⁿ⁾)*

Let's review **je voudrais et nous voudrions et** learn **avoir. Répétez** each sentence out loud. *(zhuh)(voo-dray) (new) (voo-dree-oh⁽ⁿ⁾) (ah-vwahr)(ray-pay-tay)*
I would like   we   would like   to have

Je voudrais un verre de bière. *(voo-dray) (zuh⁽ⁿ⁾)(vair) (duh) (bee-air)*   **J'ai un verre de bière.** *(zhay)*

Nous voudrions deux verres de vin. *(voo-dree-oh⁽ⁿ⁾) (duh) (va⁽ⁿ⁾)*   **Nous avons deux verres de vin.** *(ah-voh⁽ⁿ⁾)*

Je voudrais un verre d'eau. *(doe)*   **Nous avons une maison.** *(zewn)*

Nous voudrions une salade. *(zewn) (sah-lahd)*   **J'ai une maison en Amérique.** *(ah⁽ⁿ⁾)(nah-may-reek)*

Nous voudrions avoir une auto. *(zah-vwahr) (oh-toe)*   **J'ai une auto.** *(oh-toe)*

Nous voudrions avoir une auto   **Nous avons une auto en Europe.** *(ah⁽ⁿ⁾)(nuh-rope)*
en Europe. *(uh-rope)*

Now fill in the following blanks **avec** the **forme correcte** of **"avoir" ou "vouloir."** *(form) (ko-rekt)* *(oo)*
or

_____ *Nous avons* _____   **trois autos.**
 (we   have)

_____   **deux tickets d'autobus.**
 (we   would   like)

_____   **un tableau.**
 (I   have)

_____   **sept cartes postales.**
 (I   would   like)

☐ **déjà** *(day-zhah)* . . . . already   _____
 — **déjà vu** *(day-zhah vew)* . . . . already seen   _____
☐ **le désir** *(day-zeer)* . . . . desire   _____
☐ **la distance** *(dee-stah⁽ⁿ⁾-s)* . . . . distance   _____
☐ **le docteur** *(doke-tur)* . . . . doctor   _____

15

Voilà a quick review of the **couleurs.** *(koo-luhr)* Draw lines between **les mots français et les** *(lay) (mow) (frah⁽ⁿ⁾-say)*

couleurs correctes. *(ko-rekt)* On your mark, get set, *GO!*

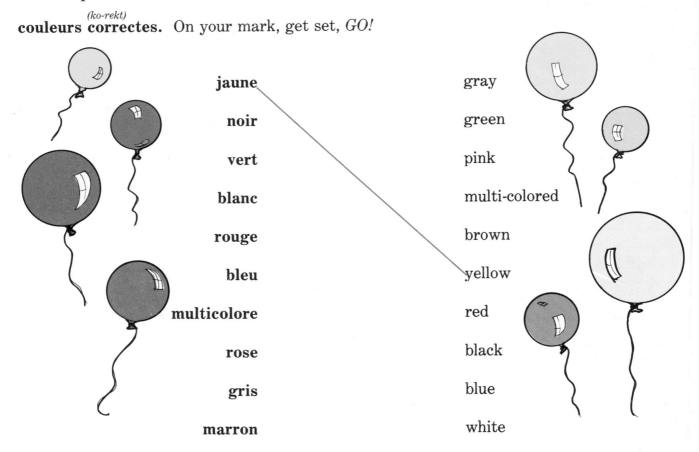

jaune	gray
noir	green
vert	pink
blanc	multi-colored
rouge	brown
bleu	yellow
multicolore	red
rose	black
gris	blue
marron	white

Where to place the accent in French need never be a problem. **Les mots français** are *(lay)* *(frah⁽ⁿ⁾-say)*

always accented on the last syllable. It's easy!

☐ **l'économie** *(lay-koh-noh-mee)* . . . . economy _____
☐ **l'entrée** *(lah⁽ⁿ⁾-tray)* . . . . entry _____
☐ **est** *(est)* . . . . east _____
☐ **l'état** *(lay-tah)* . . . . state _____
— **Les Etats-Unis d'Amérique** *(lay-zay-tah-zoo-nee dah-may-reek)* The United States of America

(lar-zhah⁽ⁿ⁾)
L'Argent
money

Before starting this Step, go back **et** review Step 4. Make sure you can count to **vingt** $^{(va^{(n)})}$

without looking back at **le livre.** $^{(lee\text{-}vruh)}$ Let's learn the larger **nombres** $^{(nome\text{-}bruh)}$ now, so if something

costs more than 20 **F** $^{(frah^{(n)})}$ you will know exactly **combien** $^{(kohm\text{-}bee\text{-}yen)}$ it costs. After practicing aloud

les nombres français 10 à 100 below, write these **nombres** in the blanks provided.

Again, notice the **similarités** $^{(see\text{-}mee\text{-}lahr\text{-}ee\text{-}tay)}$ between **nombres** such as **quatre** (4), $^{(kah\text{-}truh)}$ **quatorze** (14) $^{(kah\text{-}torz)}$ and

quarante (40). $^{(kah\text{-}rah^{(n)}t)}$

10	**dix** $^{(dees)}$	(quatre + six = dix)	10 _dix_
20	**vingt** $^{(va^{(n)})}$	(deux = 2)	20 _____
30	**trente** $^{(trah^{(n)}t)}$	(t̲r̲ois = 3)	30 _____
40	**quarante** $^{(kah\text{-}rah^{(n)}t)}$	(q̲u̲atre = 4)	40 _____
50	**cinquante** $^{(sang\text{-}kah^{(n)}t)}$	(c̲i̲n̲q = 5)	50 _____
60	**soixante** $^{(swah\text{-}sah^{(n)}t)}$	(s̲i̲x̲ = 6)	60 _____
70	**soixante-dix** (60+10) $^{(swah\text{-}sah^{(n)}t\text{-}dees)}$	(sept = 7)	70 _____
80	**quatre-vingts** (4x20) $^{(kah\text{-}truh\text{-}va^{(n)})}$	(huit = 8)	80 _____
90	**quatre-vingt-dix** (4x20+10) $^{(kah\text{-}truh\text{-}va^{(n)}\text{-}dees)}$	(neuf = 9)	90 _____
100	**cent** $^{(sah^{(n)})}$		100 _____
1000	**mille** $^{(meel)}$		1000 _____

Now take a logical guess. **Comment** $^{(ko\text{-}mah^{(n)})}$ would you write (**et** say) the following? **Les réponses** $^{(ray\text{-}poh^{(n)}s)}$

sont at the bottom of **la page.** $^{(lah)\,(pahzh)}$
are

400 _____   600 _____

2000 _____   5300 _____

The unit of currency **en France** *(ay)* **est le franc** *(frah⁽ⁿ⁾)* **français,** *(frah⁽ⁿ⁾-say)* abbreviated **F**. Bills are called **billets** *(bee-ay)* **et** coins are called **monnaie.** *(mo-nay)* Just as **un dollar américain** *(uh⁽ⁿ⁾)(doe-lahr)(ah-may-ree-ka⁽ⁿ⁾)* can be broken down into 100 pennies, **un franc français** *(frah⁽ⁿ⁾)* can be broken down into 100 **centimes.** *(sah⁽ⁿ⁾-teem)* A coin is called **une pièce de monnaie** *(ewn)(pea-ess)(mo-nay)* **et** bills can also be referred to as **papier-monnaie.** *(pah-pee-ay mo-nay)* Let's learn the various kinds of **billets et monnaie.** *(bee-ay)(mo-nay)* Always be sure to practice each **mot** out loud. You might want to exchange some money **maintenant** *(ma⁽ⁿ⁾-tuh-nah⁽ⁿ⁾)* now so that you can familiarize yourself **avec** the various types of **argent.** *(ar-zhah⁽ⁿ⁾)* money

Billets

un billet de dix francs *(uh⁽ⁿ⁾)(bee-ay)(dee)(frah⁽ⁿ⁾)*
10   francs

un billet de cinquante francs *(sang-kah⁽ⁿ⁾t)*
50

un billet de cent francs

un billet de cinq cents francs

Monnaie

une pièce d'un centime *(ewn)(pea-ess)(duh⁽ⁿ⁾)(sah⁽ⁿ⁾-teem)*
1   centime

une pièce de cinq centimes
5

une pièce de dix centimes
10

une pièce de vingt centimes

**une pièce de cinquante centimes
(un demi-franc)**

une pièce d'un franc

une pièce de cinq francs

une pièce de dix francs

☐ **la fatigue** *(fah-teeg)*	fatigue, tiredness	_____
—**je suis fatigué** *(zhuh swee fah-tee-gay)*	I am tired	_____
☐ **la fête** *(feht)*	feast, festival	_____
☐ **le festival** *(feh-stee-vahl)*	festival	_____
☐ **le film** *(feelm)*	film	_____

Review **les nombres dix** through **mille** again. **Maintenant,** *(ma^{(n)}-tuh-nah^{(n)})* how do you say "twenty-two"

(oo) **ou** "fifty-three" *(ah^{(n)})* **en français?** You basically put **les nombres** together in a logical

sequence, for example 78 (60 + 18) = **soixante-dix-huit.** *(60)* *(18, soh^{(n)})* See if you can say **et** write

out **les nombres** on this **page. Les réponses sont** *(soh^{(n)})* at the bottom of **la page.**

a. 25 = _____ (20 + 5)

b. 36 = _____ (30 + 6)

c. 47 = _____ (40 + 7)

d. 93 = _____ (4 x 20 + 13)

e. 84 = _____ (4 x 20 + 4)

f. 68 = *soixante-huit* (60 + 8)

g. 51 = _____ (50 + 1)

h. 72 = _____ (60 + 12)

To ask what something costs **en français,** one asks, **"Combien est-ce que ça coûte?"** *(kohm-bee-yen) (ess-kuh) (sah) (koot)*

Maintenant *(ma^{(n)}-tuh-nah^{(n)})* answer the following questions based on **les nombres** in parentheses.

1. **Combien est-ce que ça coûte?** *(kohm-bee-yen) (ess-kuh) (sah) (koot)*
   how much   does   it   cost
   Ça coûte *(sah) (koot)* *dix* _____ francs..
   it   costs   (10)

2. **Combien est-ce que ça coûte?**
   Ça coûte _____ francs.
   (20)

3. **Combien coûte le livre?** *(lee-vruh)*
   how much   costs
   Ça coûte _____ francs.
   (17)

4. **Combien coûte l'auto?** *(low-toe)*
   Ça coûte _____ francs.
   (2000)

5. **Combien coûte le film?** *(feelm)*
   Ça coûte _____ francs.
   (5)

6. **Combien coûte la chambre?** *(shah^{(n)}-bruh)*
   Ça coûte _____ francs.
   (24)

7. **Combien coûte le tableau?** *(tah-blow)*
   Ça coûte _____ francs.
   (923)

RÉPONSES		
		Congratulations!
a. **vingt-cinq**	1. **dix**	7. **neuf cent vingt-trois**
b. **trente-six**	2. **vingt**	6. **vingt-quatre**
c. **quarante-sept**	h. **soixante-douze**	5. **cinq**
d. **quatre-vingt-treize**	g. **cinquante et un**	4. **deux mille**
e. **quatre-vingt-quatre**	f. **soixante-huit**	3. **dix-sept**

19

Step 7

(oh-zhoor-dwee) (duh-ma(n)) (ee-air)
Aujourd'hui, demain et hier
today · tomorrow · yesterday

(kah-lah(n)-dree-ay)
Le calendrier
calendar

(suh-men) (ah) (zhoor)
Une semaine a sept jours.
week · has · days

lundi	mardi	mercredi	jeudi	vendredi	samedi	dimanche
1	2	3	4	5	6	7

(eel) (tray) (za(n)-por-tah(n))
Il est très important to know the days of the week **et** the various parts of the day.
it is very

Let's learn them. Be sure to say them aloud before filling in the blanks below. **Les**
the

(frah(n)-say)
Français begin counting their week on Monday with **lundi.**
French

(lun-dee) **lundi** _lundi_	(mar-dee) **mardi** _____
(mare-kruh-dee) **mercredi** _____	(zhuh-dee) **jeudi** _____
(vah(n)-druh-dee) **vendredi** _____	(sahm-dee) **samedi** _____
(dee-mah(n)sh) **dimanche** _____	

(oh-zhoor-dwee) (duh-ma(n)) (ee-air)(ay-tay)
If **aujourd'hui est mercredi,** then **demain est jeudi et hier était mardi. Maintenant,**
was

you supply **les réponses correctes.** If **aujourd'hui est lundi,** then **demain est** _____

et hier était _____. **Ou,** if **aujourd'hui est lundi,** then _____ **est**

mardi et _hier_ **était dimanche.** (kel) (zhoor) (ess) **Quel jour est-ce aujourd'hui? Aujourd'hui**
what day is it

(ay)
est _____.

(ma(n)-tuh-nah(n))
Maintenant, peel off the next **sept** labels **et** put them on a (kah-lah(n)-dree-ay) **calendrier** you use every day.

From **aujourd'hui** on, Monday **est "lundi."**

☐ **le filtre** (feel-truh)	filter	_____
—**un café filtre** (kah-fay feel-truh)	filtered coffee	_____
☐ **la fin** (fa(n))	end	_____
☐ **le fontionnaire** (foh(n)-see-oh-nair)......	functionary, civil servant	_____
☐ **le football** (foot-bahl)	soccer	_____

20

There are **quatre** parts to each **jour**.
day

morning = **matin** _(ma-ta(n))_

afternoon = **après-midi** _(ah-pray-mee-dee)_

evening = **soir** _(swahr)_ _soir, soir, soir, soir, soir_

night = **nuit** _(nwee)_

Notice that the French days of the week are not capitalized as **en anglais**. **Maintenant,** _(ma(n)-tuh-nah(n))_

fill in the following blanks **et** then check your **réponses** at the bottom of **la page**.

a. Sunday morning = _dimanche matin_

b. Friday evening = _____

c. Saturday evening = _____

d. Monday morning = _____

e. Wednesday morning = _____

f. Tuesday afternoon = _____

g. Thursday afternoon = _____

h. Thursday night = _____

i. yesterday evening = _____

j. yesterday morning = _____

k. tomorrow evening = _____

l. tomorrow afternoon = _____

m. yesterday afternoon = _____

RÉPONSES

m. hier après-midi		
l. demain après-midi	h. jeudi nuit	d. lundi matin
k. demain soir	g. jeudi après-midi	c. samedi soir
j. hier matin	f. mardi après-midi	b. vendredi soir
i. hier soir	e. mercredi matin	a. dimanche matin

21

So, **avec** merely **onze mots** you can specify any day of the **semaine et** any time of the *(zhoor)* **jour.** *(suh-men)*

Les mots "**aujourd'hui**," *(oh-zhoor-dwee)* "**demain**" *(duh-ma(n))* **et** "**hier**" *(ee-air)* will be **très** *(tray)* **importants** *(za(n)-por-tah(n))* for you in making

réservations *(ray-zair-vah-see-oh(n))* **et rendez-vous,** *(rah(n)-day-voo)* in getting **billets** *(bee-yay)* **de** *(duh)* **théâtre** *(tay-ah-truh)* **et** many things you will
reservations   appointments   theater tickets

wish to do. Knowing the parts of **le jour** will help you to learn **et** understand the various

salutations *(sah-lew-tah-see-oh(n))* **françaises** *(frah(n)-sez)* below. Practice these every day now until your trip.
greetings

good morning good afternoon	=	*(boh(n)-zhoor)* **bonjour**
good evening	=	*(boh(n)-swahr)* **bonsoir**
good night	=	*(bun)* *(nwee)* **bonne nuit**
hi!	=	*(sah-lew)* **salut**

bonne nuit

Take the next **quatre** labels **et** stick them on the appropriate **choses** *(showz)* in your **maison.** *(maze-oh(n))* How
things

about the bathroom mirror **pour** *(poor)* "**bonjour**"? **Ou** the front door **pour** "**bonsoir**"? **Ou**
for

your alarm clock **pour** "**bonne nuit**"? Remember that whenever you enter small shops **et**

stores **en France** you will hear the appropriate **salutation** *(sah-lew-tah-see-oh(n))* for the time of day. Don't

be surprised. It is a **très** *(tray)* friendly **et** warm **coutume.** *(koo-tewm)* Everyone greets everyone **et** you
custom

should too, if you really want to enjoy **la France.** You **êtes** *(et)* about one-fourth of your
are

way through **le livre** *(lee-vruh)* **et c'est** *(say)* a good time to quickly review **les mots** you have learned
it is

before doing the crossword puzzle on the next **page. Amusez-vous** *(ah-mew-zay-voo)* **et bonne** *(bun)* **chance.** *(shah(n)s)* **Ou**
amuse yourself   good   luck

as we say **en anglais,** have fun and good luck.

RÉPONSES TO CROSSWORD PUZZLE (MOTS CROISÉS)

ACROSS		DOWN			
1. je voudrais	16. cinquante	1. jour	16. pourquoi		
2. avec	17. pendule	2. carte postale	17. pièce		
3. avoir	18. aujourd'hui	3. noir	18. lampe		
4. Amérique	19. lumière	4. l'après-midi	19. mur		
5. monnaie	20. eau	5. plafond	20. rouge		
6. ticket d'autobus	21. cinq	6. réponse	21. vert		
7. samedi	22. quatre	7. salut	22. vendredi		
8. banque	23. et	8. qui	23. maison		
9. dix-neuf	24. voilà	9. qu'est-ce que c'est	24. coin		
10. nuit	25. comment	10. argent	25. gris		
11. thé	26. jaune	11. femme	26. combien		
12. vingt	27. multicolore	12. un	27. quand		
13. mercredi	28. trois	13. mardi	28. deux		
14. chaise	29. tableau	14. nous avons			
15. homme	30. rideau	15. blanc			

CROSSWORD PUZZLE (MOTS CROISÉS) *(kwah-zay)*

ACROSS

1. I would like
2. with
3. to have
4. America
5. coins
6. bus ticket
7. Saturday
8. bank
9. 19
10. night
11. tea
12. 20
13. Wednesday
14. chair
15. man
16. 50
17. clock
18. today
19. light
20. water
21. five
22. four
23. and
24. there is
25. how?
26. yellow
27. multi-colored
28. three
29. picture
30. curtain

DOWN

1. day
2. postcard
3. black
4. the afternoon
5. ceiling
6. response, answer
7. hi
8. who?
9. what is it?
10. money
11. woman
12. a (masculine)
13. Tuesday
14. we have
15. white
16. why?
17. room
18. lamp
19. wall
20. red
21. green
22. Friday
23. house
24. corner
25. gray
26. how much?
27. when?
28. two

23

Step 8

(pray-poh-zee-see-oh⁽ⁿ⁾)(frah⁽ⁿ⁾-sez)

Les prépositions françaises (words like "in," "on," "through" and "next to") **sont**
_{are}

easy to learn **et** they allow you to be precise **avec** a minimum of effort. Instead of having

(sees)

to point **six** times at a piece of yummy pastry you wish to order, you can explain precisely

(eel)

which one you want by saying **il est** behind, in front of, next to, **ou** under the piece of
_{it is}

(puh-tee)

pastry which the salesperson is starting to pick up. Let's learn some of these **petits mots**
_{little}

(tray) (see-mee-lair)   *(eg-zah⁽ⁿ⁾-pluh)*

which **sont très similaires** to **anglais**. Study the **exemples** below.

(duh) **de*** = out of/from *(dah⁽ⁿ⁾)* **dans** = into/in	*(ah koh-tay duh)* **à côté de*** = next to	*(soo)* **sous** = under *(oh-duh-sue-duh)* **au-dessus de*** = over

(ah⁽ⁿ⁾-truh)   *(noo-vel) (oh-tell)*

L'homme entre dans le nouvel hôtel.
_{goes}   _{new}

(vee-a⁽ⁿ⁾)   *(lek-say-lah⁽ⁿ⁾)*

La femme vient de l'excellent hôtel.
_{comes}

(doke-tur)   *(bun)*

Le docteur est dans le bon hôtel.
_{good}

(noo-voh)

Le nouveau tableau est <u>au-dessus de</u> la table.
_{new}

(lor-lozh)

Le nouveau tableau est <u>à côté de</u> l'horloge.
_{large clock}

Le chien gris est <u>sous</u> la table marron.

(dew)

La table marron est <u>au-dessus du</u> chien.

(vairt)

L'horloge verte est <u>au-dessus de</u> la table.

L'horloge verte est <u>à côté du</u> tableau.

(de + le)   *(de + les)*

*Remember that **de** sometimes combines with **la, le** or **les** to form **du, de la, de l'** and **des**.

☐ **la forme** *(form)*	form, shape	_____
☐ **la forêt** *(foh-ray)*	forest	_____
☐ **le foyer** *(fwah-yay)*	home, hearth	_____
☐ **franc/franche** *(frah⁽ⁿ⁾/frah⁽ⁿ⁾sh)*	frank, honest	_____
☐ **le fruit** *(fwee)*	fruit	_____

Fill in the blanks below **avec les prépositions correctes** *(pray-poh-zee-see-oh⁽ⁿ⁾)* according to the **images** *(ee-mahzh)* on the previous **page**.

pictures

L'homme entre *(ah⁽ⁿ⁾-truh)* _____ **le nouvel hôtel.**

Le chien gris est *sous* **la table.**

L'horloge verte est *(lor-lozh) (vairt)* _____ **la table.**

Le docteur est _____ **le bon hôtel.**

L'horloge verte est _____ **du tableau.**

Le nouveau tableau est *(noo-voh)* _____ **la table.**

La table marron est _____ **le tableau.**

Le nouveau tableau est _____ **l'horloge.**

La femme vient *(fahm)* _____ **l'excellent hôtel.**

La table marron est _____ **l'horloge.**

Maintenant, répondez aux questions *(ma⁽ⁿ⁾-tuh-nah⁽ⁿ⁾) (oh) (kehs-tee-oh⁽ⁿ⁾)* based on **les images** *(lay) (zee-mahzh)* on the previous **page**.

to the

Où est le docteur? _____

Où est le chien? *(shee-ya⁽ⁿ⁾)* _____

Où est la table? _____

Où est le tableau? _____

Que fait la femme? *(kuh) (fay)* _____

does

Que fait l'homme? *(fay)* _____

does

L'horloge est-elle verte? *Oui, l'horloge est verte.*

is   it

Le chien est-il gris? *Oui,* _____

is   it

☐ **la glace** *(glahs)* .... ice, ice cream
☐ **la galerie** *(gah-lur-ee)* .... gallery, long room
☐ **la géographie** *(zhay-oo-grah-fee)* .... geography
☐ **la gomme** *(gohm)* .... chewing gum, eraser
☐ **le gourmand** *(gour-mah⁽ⁿ⁾)* .... gormand, glutton

_____
_____
_____
_____
_____

Maintenant for some more practice **avec les prépositions françaises.**

> *(sewr)*
> **sur** = on
>
> *(ah$^{(n)}$-truh)*
> **entre** = between
>
> *(duh-vah$^{(n)}$)*
> **devant** = in front of
>
> *(dare-ee-air)*
> **derrière** = behind

(vair) *(doe)* *(sewr)*
Le verre d'eau est sur la table.　　Le verre d'eau est _____ la table.

Le tableau multicolore est sur le mur.　Le tableau multicolore est _*sur*_ le mur.

(dare-ee-air)
La lampe jaune est derrière la table.　La lampe jaune est _____ la table.

(duh-vah$^{(n)}$) *(lee)*
La table marron est devant le lit.　　La table est _____ le lit.
　　　　　　　　　　　　　bed

(ah$^{(n)}$-truh)
La lampe jaune est entre la table et　La lampe jaune est _____ la table et
le lit.　　　　　　　　　　　　　le lit.

(oh)
Répondez aux questions, based on **les images,** by filling in the blanks **avec les**
　　　　　to the

prépositions correctes. Choose **les prépositions** from those you have just learned.

Où est le livre rouge?　　　　　Le livre rouge est _____ la table marron.

Où est l'autobus bleu?　　　　　L'autobus bleu est _____ l'hôtel gris.

☐ **le gourmet** *(gour-may)* . . . . gourmet, epicure　　_____
☐ **le gouvernement** *(goo-vair-nuh-mah$^{(n)}$)* . government　　_____
☐ **grand** *(grah$^{(n)}$)* . . . . big　　_____
☐ **la grandeur** *(grah$^{(n)}$-dur)* . . . . greatness　　_____
☐ **le guide** *(geed)* . . . . guide

Où est le téléphone *(tay-lay-phone)* *(gree)* gris? Où est le tapis *(tah-pee)* *(vair)* vert? Où est le tableau?

Le téléphone est _____ le mur blanc.

Le téléphone est _____ du tableau multicolore.

Le téléphone est *au-dessus de* la table noire.

Le tapis vert est _____ la table noire.

Le tableau est _____ le mur blanc.

Maintenant, fill in each blank on **le château** *(shah-toe)* below **avec** the best possible **préposition.**
castle

Les réponses correctes sont at the bottom of **la page. Amusez-vous.**
have fun

1. _____

2. _____

5. _____

3. _____

8. *devant*

9. _____

6. _____

7. _____

4. _____

10. _____

RÉPONSES				
1. **au-dessus de**	2. **sur**			10. **de**
3. **derrière**	4. **entre**	5. **dans**	6. **dans**	8. **devant**
		7. **à côté de**	9. **sous**	

27

Step 9

(zhah(n)-vee-ay) (fay-vree-ay) (mars)
Janvier, février, mars

(oh(n)) (sep-tah(n)m-bruh) (ah-vreel) (zhoo-a(n)) (no-vah(n)m-bruh)
Trente jours ont septembre, avril, juin et novembre . . .
have

(suh-men) (mow-mah(n))
Sound familiar? You have learned the days of **la semaine,** so **maintenant c'est le moment**
it is

(mwah) (duh) (lah-nay) (tah(n))
to learn **les mois de l'année et** all kinds of **temps** which you might encounter on your
months of the year weather

(eg-zah(n)-pluh) (tah(n))
holiday. For **exemple,** you ask about **le temps en français** just as you would **en anglais—**

(kel) (fay-teel) (kehs-tee-oh(n))
"Quel temps fait-il aujourd'hui?" Practice all the possible answers to this **question**
what weather does it do today

(pwee)
et puis write **les réponses** in the blanks below.
then

(kel) (tah(n)) (fay-teel) (oh-zhoor-dwee)
Quel temps fait-il aujourd'hui?

(eel) (pluh)
Il pleut aujourd'hui. _____
rains

(nehzh)
Il neige aujourd'hui. *Il neige aujourd'hui.*
snows

(fay) (fray)
Il fait frais aujourd'hui. _____
cool

(fwah)
Il fait froid aujourd'hui. _____
cold

(boh)
Il fait beau aujourd'hui. _____
nice

(mow-vay)
Il fait mauvais aujourd'hui. _____
bad

(show)
Il fait chaud aujourd'hui. _____
hot

(dew) (broo-ee-yar)
Il fait du brouillard aujourd'hui. _____
foggy

(pwee)
Maintenant, practice **les mots** on the next **page** aloud **et puis** fill in the blanks with
then

(noh(n)) (mwah)
les noms of **les mois et** the appropriate weather report. Notice that **en français,** the
names months

months of the year and the days of the week are not capitalized.

☐ **l'identification** *(lee-dah(n)-tee-fee-kah-see-oh(n))* . identification _____
☐ **l'île** *(leel)* . . . . island _____
☐ **l'importance** *(la(n)-por-tah(n)s)* . . . . importance _____
— **une chose importante** *(a(n)-por-tah(n)t)* . . . . an important thing _____
28 ☐ **inacceptable** *(een-ahk-sep-tahb-luh)* . . . . unacceptable _____

(ah⁽ⁿ⁾)(zhah⁽ⁿ⁾-vee-ay)
en janvier _____
in

(nehzh)
Il neige en janvier. _____

(fay-vree-ay)
en février _____

(oh-see)
Il neige aussi en février. _____
also

(mars)
en mars *en mars*

(pluh)
Il pleut en mars. _____

(ah-vreel)
en avril _____

Il pleut aussi en avril. _____

(may)
en mai _____

(fay) (dew) (vah⁽ⁿ⁾)
Il fait du vent en mai. _____
windy

(zhoo-a⁽ⁿ⁾)
en juin _____

(so-lay)
Il fait du soleil en juin. _____
sunny

(zhwee-ay)
en juillet _____

(boh)
Il fait beau en juillet. _____

(oot)
en août _____

(show)
Il fait chaud en août. *Il fait chaud en août.*

(sep-tah⁽ⁿ⁾m-bruh)
en septembre _____

(broo-ee-yar)
Il fait du brouillard en septembre. _____
foggy

(ok-toh-bruh)
en octobre _____

(fray)
Il fait frais en octobre. _____

(no-vah⁽ⁿ⁾m-bruh)
en novembre _____

(mow-vay)
Il fait mauvais en novembre. _____

(day-sah⁽ⁿ⁾m-bruh)
en décembre _____

Il fait froid en décembre. _____

Maintenant, répondez aux questions based on **les images** to the right.

Quel temps fait-il en février? *Il fait* _____
in

Quel temps fait-il en avril? _____

Quel temps fait-il en mai? _____

Quel temps fait-il en août? _____

Quel temps fait-il aujourd'hui, beau ou mauvais? _____

☐ **impossible** *(a⁽ⁿ⁾-poh-see-bluh)* . . . . impossible
  — C'est impossible! *(say ta⁽ⁿ⁾-poh-see-bluh)* . . It's impossible!
☐ **l'industrie** *(la⁽ⁿ⁾-dew-stree)* . . . . industry
☐ **l'information** *(la⁽ⁿ⁾-for-mah-see-oh⁽ⁿ⁾)* . . . . . . information
☐ **l'ingénieur** *(la⁽ⁿ⁾-zhay-nee-ur)* . . . . engineer

_____
_____
_____
_____

29

Maintenant, les *(say-zoh(n))* saisons de l'année . . .
seasons

(lee-vair) **l'hiver** winter

(lay-tay) **l'été** summer

(loh-tone) **l'automne** autumn

(pra(n)-tah(n)) **le printemps** spring

l'été

| **Il fait froid** *(ah(n))(nee-vair)* **en hiver.** | **Il fait chaud** *(ah(n))(nay-tay)* **en été.** | **Il fait du vent** *(ah(n))(noh-tone)* **en automne.** | **Il pleut** *(oh)* **au printemps.** |

At this point, *(say)* **c'est** *(tewn)* **une** *(bun)* **bonne** *(ee-day)* **idée** to familiarize yourself **avec les** *(tah(n)-pay-rah-tewr)* **températures**
it is   a   good   idea   temperatures

(uh-roh-pay-yen) **européennes.** Carefully read the typical weather forecasts below **et** study **le thermomètre** *(tair-moh-meh-truh)*
European   thermometer

because **les températures en** *(uh-rope)* **Europe** are calculated on the basis of Centigrade (not

Fahrenheit).

Fahrenheit	**Celsius**	
212° F ——	100° C	*(low)* *(boo)* **l'eau bout** boils
98.6° F ——	37° C	**la température normale du sang** of blood
68° F ——	20° C	
32° F ——	0° C	**l'eau douce gèle** water fresh freezes
0° F ——	-17.8° C	**l'eau salée gèle** water salt freezes
-10° F ——	-23.3° C	

Le temps pour lundi 21 mars:

> **froid avec du vent**
>
> **température: 5 degrés** *(duh-gray)*
> degrees

Le temps pour mardi 18 juillet:

> **beau et chaud**
>
> **température: 20 degrés**

(fwah-yay) *(fa⁽ⁿ⁾)* *(fwah)*
Foyer, faim et foi
home · hunger · faith

Just as we have the 3 "R's" **en anglais, en français** there are the 3 "F's" which help us to understand some of the basics of **la** *(vee)* **vie** *(frah⁽ⁿ⁾-sez)* **française.**
life · French

Foyer · **F**aim · **F**oi

Study **les images** below **et** *(pwee)* **puis** write out **les** *(noo-voh)* **nouveaux mots** in the blanks which follow.
new

(lahr-bruh) *(zhay-nay-ah-loh-zheek)*
L'Arbre généalogique
tree · genealogical

(mee-shell)
Michel Roquefort
(Monsieur Roquefort)

(kloh-deen) *(rowk-for)*
Claudine Roquefort
(Madame Roquefort)

(fee-leep) *(mee-too)*
Philippe Mitou

(mah-ree frah⁽ⁿ⁾s)
Marie-France Mitou

(bear-trah⁽ⁿ⁾)
Bertrand Roquefort

(dah-nee-el)
Danielle Roquefort

(fah-mee-yah)
la famille
family

(nee-ko-lah)
Nicolas

(kah-roh-leen)
Caroline

☐ **la jaquette** *(zhah-ket)*	woman's jacket	_____
☐ **le Japon** *(zhah-poh⁽ⁿ⁾)*	Japan	_____
— **japonais** *(zhah-poh-nay)*	Japanese	_____
☐ **le journal** *(zhoor-nahl)*	newspaper	_____
☐ **La Joconde** *(zhoh-kohnd)*	Mona Lisa in the Louvre	_____

31

(grah⁽ⁿ⁾-pah-rah⁽ⁿ⁾)
les grands-parents
grandparents

(pah-rah⁽ⁿ⁾)
les parents
parents

(grah⁽ⁿ⁾-pear)
le grand-père   *le grand-père*
grandfather

(pear)
le père _____
father

(grah⁽ⁿ⁾-mare)
la grand-mère _____
grandmother

(mare)
la mère _____
mother

(lay) (zah⁽ⁿ⁾-fah⁽ⁿ⁾)
les enfants
children

(pah-rah⁽ⁿ⁾)
les parents
relatives

(fees)
le fils _____
son

(loh⁽ⁿ⁾-kluh)
l'oncle _____
uncle

(fee-yah)
la fille _____
daughter

(taunt)
la tante _____
aunt

Le fils et la fille sont aussi frère et soeur.
                                    (frair)   *(suhr)*
                                    brother   sister

Let's learn how to identify **la famille** by **nom.** Study the following **exemples.**
                          (fah-mee-yah)   *(noh⁽ⁿ⁾)*
                          family   name

Comment s'appelle le père?
how *(sah-pell)* the father
    is called

Comment s'appelle la mère?
                    is called

Le père s'appelle *Bertrand*.
       is called

La mère s'appelle *Danielle*.
       is called

Maintenant you fill in the following blanks, **basés sur les images,** in the same manner.
                                            (bah-zay) (sewr)
                                            based   on

Comment s'appelle *le fils* ?

Comment s'appelle _____ ?

_____ **s'appelle** _____.

_____ **s'appelle** _____.

☐ **juste** *(zhoost)* . . . .   fair, just   _____
☐ **la justice** *(zhoo-stees)* . . . .   justice   _____
☐ **le kilomètre** *(kee-loh-meh-truh)* . . . .   kilometer (= .624 miles)   _____
☐ **le kiosque** *(kee-ohsk)* . . . .   kiosk   _____
☐ **le kilo** *(kee-loh)* . . . .   kilo (= 2.2 pounds)   _____

(kwee-zeen)
La cuisine
kitchen

Study all these **images et puis** practice

saying **et** writing out **les mots.**

^(lah)
Voilà la cuisine.

(ray-free-zhay-rah-tuhr)
le réfrigérateur

_____

(kwee-zee-nee-air)
la cuisinière
stove

_____

(va⁽ⁿ⁾)
le vin

_____

(bee-air)
la bière

_____

^(lay)
le lait

le lait

_____

(buhr)
le beurre

_____

Répondez aux questions aloud.

Où est la bière? . . . . **La bière est dans le réfrigérateur.**
(ray-free-zhay-rah-tuhr)

^(luh)
Où est le lait?   **Où est le vin?**   **Où est le beurre?**

☐ **le lac** *(lack)* . . . . lake   _____
☐ **le langage** *(lah⁽ⁿ⁾-gahzh)* . . . . language   _____
☐ **la leçon** *(lay-soh⁽ⁿ⁾)* . . . . lesson   _____
☐ **la lecture** *(lek-tewr)* . . . . reading   _____
☐ **la liberté** *(lee-bear-tay)* . . . . liberty   _____

33

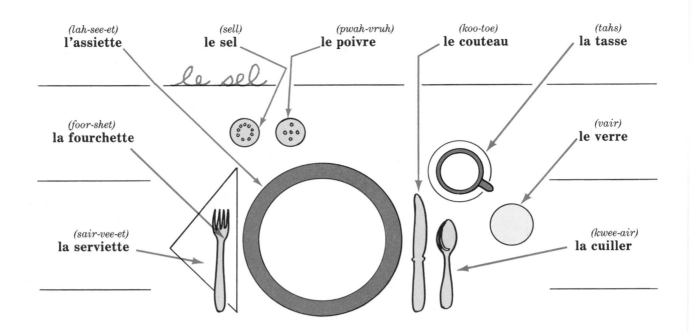

(lah-see-et) **l'assiette**

(sell) **le sel**

(pwah-vruh) **le poivre**

(koo-toe) **le couteau**

(tahs) **la tasse**

le sel

(foor-shet) **la fourchette**

(vair) **le verre**

(sair-vee-et) **la serviette**

(kwee-air) **la cuiller**

(plah-kar) **le placard**

(pa(n)) **le pain**

(tay) **le thé**

(kah-fay) **le café**

le thé

Où est le pain? Le pain est dans le placard. Où est le thé? Où est le café? Où est le sel? Où est le poivre? Maintenant ouvrez *(oo-vray)* _{open} your **livre** to the **page avec** the labels **et** remove the next **dix-neuf** labels **et** proceed to label all these **choses** in your **maison.** Do not forget to use every opportunity to say these **mots** out loud. **C'est** *(say)* **très important!** *(a(n)-por-tah(n))*

☐ **le lieu** *(lee-uh)* . . . . place
☐ **la ligne** *(leen-yuh)* . . . . line
☐ **la limonade** *(lee-mow-nod)* . . . . lemonade
☐ **le logement** *(lozh-mah(n))* . . . . lodging
☐ **Londres** *(loh(n)-druh)* . . . . London

34

En France, there is not the wide variety of **religions** *(ruh-lee-zhee-oh⁽ⁿ⁾)* that **nous avons ici en Amérique.**
religions   we   have

A person's **religion est généralement** *(ruh-lee-zhee-oh⁽ⁿ⁾)* *(zhay-nay-rahl-mah⁽ⁿ⁾)* one of the following.
generally

1. **catholique** *(kah-toe-leek)* _catholique_
   Catholic

2. **protestant** *(pro-teh-stah⁽ⁿ⁾)* _____
   Protestant

3. **juif** *(zhew-eef)* _____
   Jewish

4. **musulman** *(mew-zewl-mah⁽ⁿ⁾)* _____
   Moslem

Voilà une cathédrale en France. *(kah-tay-drahl)*
cathedral

Est-ce une cathédrale catholique

ou protestante? *(pro-teh-stah⁽ⁿ⁾t)** **Est-ce une nouvelle**

cathédrale? Non, **c'est une vieille** *(say)* *(vee-ay)*
old

cathédrale. You will see **beaucoup** *(boh-koo)*
many

de belles cathédrales *(bell)* like this during
beautiful

your holiday **en France.**

Maintenant let's learn how to say "I am" **en français:** I am = **je suis** *(zhuh) (swee)* _____

Practice saying **"je suis" avec** the following **mots. Maintenant** write each sentence for

more practice.

Je suis catholique. _____   **Je suis protestant.** _____

Je suis juif. _Je suis juif._   **Je suis américain.** _____

Je suis en Europe. *(uh-rope)* _____   **Je suis en France.** _____

*To make an adjective feminine **en français,** all you usually need to do is to add an "e." This will sometimes vary the pronunciation slightly.

☐ **le magasin** *(ma-gah-za⁽ⁿ⁾)* . . . . store _____
☐ **le magazine** *(ma-gah-zeen)* . . . . magazine _____
☐ **magnifique** *(mahn-ee-feek)* . . . . magnificent _____
☐ **le marchand** *(mar-shah⁽ⁿ⁾)* . . . . merchant _____
☐ **le mécanicien** *(may-kah-nee-see-a⁽ⁿ⁾)* . . . . mechanic _____

35

Je suis dans l'église. _____   Je suis dans la cuisine. _____

(dah⁽ⁿ⁾) — in (above "dans")

Je suis la mère. *Je suis la mère.*   Je suis le père. _____

Je suis dans l'hôtel. _____   Je suis dans le restaurant. _____

Je suis fatigué. _____   Je suis à côté de l'église. _____

(fah-tee-gay) (above "fatigué")

Maintenant identify all **les personnes dans le tableau** below. On the **lignes,** write **le mot correct en français** for the **personne** corresponding to **le nombre sous l'image.**

(pear-sohn) — people (above "personnes")
(leen-yuh) — lines (above "lignes")

1. _____   2. _____

3. _____   4. _____

5. *la tante*   6. _____

7. _____

Don't be afraid of all of the extra hyphens, apostrophes, accents and uncommon squiggles in French. Concentrate on your easy pronunciation guide and, remember - practice, practice, practice.

est-ce = *(ess)*	**qu'est-ce que c'est** = *(kess-kuh-say)*	**s'appelle** = *(sah-pel)*
is it	what is that?	is called

☐ **le marché** *(mar-shay)* . . . . market	_____
— **bon marché** *(boh⁽ⁿ⁾ mar-shay)* . . . . cheap	_____
☐ **le mariage** *(mar-ee-ahzh)* . . . . marriage, wedding	_____
☐ **le médicament** *(may-dee-kah-mah⁽ⁿ⁾)* . . . . . . medicine	_____
☐ **la mer** *(mare)* . . . . sea	_____

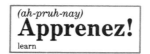

(ah-pruh-nay)
Apprenez!
learn

(voo)
Vous have already used the verbs **avoir** *(ah-vwahr)* and **voudrais** *(voo-dray)*, **coûter** *(koo-tay)*, **arriver** *(ah-ree-vay)*, **entrer** *(ah^(n)-tray)*, **venir** *(vuh-neer)*,
you
to cost

(ray-poh^(n)-druh)(ray-pay-tay) (ay) *(swee)*
répondre, répéter, est, sont and **suis.** Although you might be able to "get by" **avec**

(vairb) *(mee-yuh)*
these **verbes,** let's assume you want to do **mieux** than that. First, a quick review.
better

How do you say "I" **en français?** *je* How do you say "we" **en français?** _____

Compare these **deux** charts

(ah-pruh-nay)
very carefully **et apprenez** these
learn

sept mots on the right.

	(zhuh)			*(new)*
I =	**je**		we =	**nous**
	(eel)			*(voo)*
he/it =	**il**		you =	**vous**
	(el)			*(eel)*
she/it =	**elle**		they =	**ils** (masculine)
				(el)
			they =	**elles** (feminine)

(leen-yuh) (ah^(n)-truh)
Maintenant draw **lignes entre** the matching **mots anglais et mots français** below to see
between

if you can keep these **mots** straight in your mind.

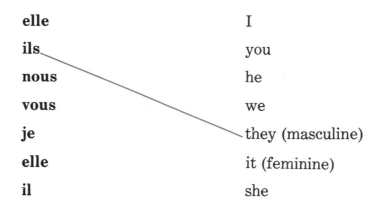

elle   I

ils   you

nous   he

vous   we

je   they (masculine)

elle   it (feminine)

il   she

(ewn) (fuh-yuh)
Maintenant close **le livre et** write out both columns of the above practice on **une feuille**

(pah-pee-ay) *(bee-ya^(n))* *(mahl)* *(pah)* *(voo)*
de papier. How did **vous** do? **Bien ou mal? Pas bien, pas mal? Maintenant** that **vous**
well poorly not too well not too bad

(kuh) *(day-zee-ray)*
know these **mots,** you will soon be able to say almost anything **que vous désirez** by using
that desire

a type of "plug-in" formula.

☐ **le métropolitain** *(may-tro-poh-lee-ta^(n))* . . .	subway (metro!)	_____
☐ **la minute** *(mee-newt)*	minute	_____
— **la minuterie** *(mee-new-tuh-ree)*	automatic light switch	_____
☐ **la mode** *(mode)*	fashion	_____
— **à la mode**	fashionable	_____

To demonstrate, here are *(seez)* **six exemples** of very practical **et** important **verbes français.**

These are **verbes** whose basic form ends in **"er."** Write **les verbes** in the blanks below

after **vous** have practiced them out loud many times.

(par-lay)
parler = to speak

(reh-stay)
rester = to remain/stay

(ah-bee-tay)
habiter = to live/reside

_____

rester

_____

(ko-mah⁽ⁿ⁾-day)
commander = to order

(ah-shuh-tay)
acheter = to buy

(saw-puh-lay)
s'appeler = to be called

_____

_____

_____

Study the following verb patterns **avec attention.**

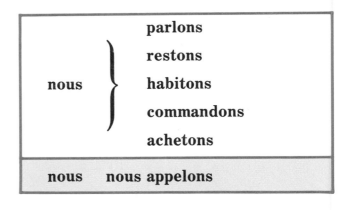

je / il / elle	parle
	reste
	habite
	commande
	achète

je	m'appelle
il/elle	s'appelle

nous	parlons
	restons
	habitons
	commandons
	achetons

nous	nous appelons

Note: • With **je, il,** or **elle** you drop the final "r" from the basic verb form.

   • With **nous** you drop the final "er" of the basic verb form and substitute "ons"

   in its place. **Exemple: nous parlons.** *(par-loh⁽ⁿ⁾)*
   we   speak

   • **S'appeler** varies but not too much. It is a very important verb so take a few

   extra minutes to learn it.

Some **verbes en français** will not conform to rules quite as easily as these **verbes** do. But

don't worry . . . you will be perfectly understood whether you say **"parle"** or **"parlons."**

Les Français will be delighted that you have taken the time to learn their language.

☐ **le monde** *(mohnd)* . . . . world   _____
 — **tout le monde** *(too luh mohnd)* . . . . everyone   _____
☐ **la montagne** *(moh⁽ⁿ⁾-tahn-yuh)* . . . . mountain   _____
☐ **le musée** *(mew-zay)* . . . . museum   _____
38 ☐ **la musique** *(mew-zeek)* . . . . music   _____

Important! Concentrate on the **similarités** *(see-mee-lar-ee-tay)* of pronunciation **en français** rather than on the spelling. It's really much easier than it looks.

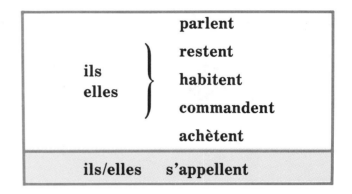

Here are a few hints for mixing and matching verbs and their subjects.

-ons ⟶ nous ex. **nous parlons**   -ent ⟶ ils ex. **ils parlent**
                                             elles ex. **elles parlent**
-ez ⟶ vous ex. **vous parlez**

Maintenant, read through the entire verb form aloud several times before writing out each form in its blank. Notice in the first pattern, how despite the difference in spelling, the verbs are pronounced the same (*).

parler

Je* *parle/* _____ français.

Il* *parle/* _____ français.
Elle

Nous *parlons/* _____ français.

Vous *parlez/* _____ anglais.

Ils* *parlent/* _____ anglais.
Elles

rester

Je* *reste/* _____ en France.

Il* *reste/* _____ en Amérique.
Elle

Nous *restons/* _____ dans un hôtel.

Vous *restez/* _____ en Europe.

Ils* *restent/* _____ en Belgique.
Elles

☐ **la nation** *(nah-see-oh⁽ⁿ⁾)* . . . . nation
☐ **la nature** *(nah-tewr)* . . . . nature
☐ **naturel** *(nah-tew-rel)* . . . . natural
  — **au naturel** *(oh nah-tew-rel)* . . . . plain, simple
☐ **la nécessité** *(nay-say-see-tay)* . . . . necessity

_____
_____
_____
_____
_____

habiter

J' *habite* _____ en France.

Il _____ en Amérique.
Elle

Nous_____en Italie.

Vous_____en Europe.

Ils _____en Chine.
Elles

acheter

J' *achète* _____ un livre.

Il _____ une salade.
Elle

Nous _____ une auto.

Vous _____ une horloge.

Ils _____ une lampe.
Elles

s'appeler

Je _____ Jeanne Guégan.

Il _____Mitou.
Elle

Nous _____ Smith.

Vous _____ Thierry Huck.

Ils _____Roquefort.
Elles

commander

Je _____ un verre d'eau.

Il _____ un verre de vin.
Elle

Nous _____ une tasse de thé.

Vous _____ une tasse de café.

Ils _____ un verre de lait.
Elles

Remember these **verbes?**

(vuh-neer)
venir = to come

(ah-lay)
aller = to go

(ah-prah$^{(n)}$-druh)
apprendre = to learn

venir _____

_____

_____

(voo-dray)
voudrais = would like

(ah-vwahr)
avoir = to have

(buh-zwa$^{(n)}$)
avoir besoin de = to need
to have   need   of

_____

_____

_____

Here we have **six,** already familiar **verbes** whose following forms might seem a bit erratic

after our last group. DON'T PANIC or give up. Read them out loud, practice them, think

of their **similarités,** write them out and then try to use them in sentences of your own.

☐ **neuf** *(nuf)*	new	_____
— **Le Pont Neuf à Paris** *(poh$^{(n)}$ nuf)*	new bridge in Paris (1604)	_____
☐ **Noël** *(no-el)*	Christmas	_____
☐ **le nord** *(nor)*	north	_____
☐ **Notre-Dame de Paris** *(no-truh dahm)*	Our Lady (cathedral)	

40

Think of how hard it would be to speak **en anglais** with no verbs — it's the same **en français.**

venir

Je _viens/_ _____ de l'Amérique.

Il _vient/_ _____ de la Belgique.
Elle

Nous _venons/_ _____ du Canada.

Vous _venez/_ _____ de New York.

Ils _viennent/_ _____ de la Suisse.
Elles

aller

Je _vais/_ _____ en France.

Il _va/_ _____ en Italie.
Elle

Nous _allons/_ _____ en Angleterre.

Vous _allez/_ _____ en Europe.

Ils _vont/_ _____ en Chine.
Elles

apprendre

J' _apprends/_ _____ le français.

Il _apprend/_ _____ l'anglais.
Elle

Nous _apprenons/_ _____ la géometrie.

Vous _apprenez/_ _____ l'allemand.

Ils _apprennent/_ _____ l'espagnol.
Elles

voudrais / voudrions

Je _voudrais/_ _____ un verre de vin.

Il _voudrait/_ _____ un verre de vin rouge.
Elle

Nous _voudrions_ _____ un verre de vin blanc.

Vous _voudriez/_ _____ un verre de lait.

Ils _voudraient/_ _____ un verre de bière.
Elles

avoir

J' _ai/_ _____ cinq francs.

Il _a/_ _____ six francs.
Elle

Nous _avons/_ _____ dix francs.

Vous _avez/_ _____ deux francs.

Ils _ont/_ _____ trois francs.
Elles

avoir besoin de

J' _ai besoin_ _____ d'un verre de vin.

Il _____ d'un verre de vin rouge.
Elle

Nous _____ d'un verre de vin blanc.

Vous _____ d'un verre de lait.

Ils _____ d'un verre de bière.
Elles

☐ **l'objet** *(lobe-zhay)* . . . . object
☐ **obligatoire** *(oh-blee-gah-twahr)* . . . . compulsory
☐ **l'observation** *(lobe-sair-vah-see-oh⁽ⁿ⁾)* . . . . observation
☐ **l'occupation** *(low-kew-pah-see-oh⁽ⁿ⁾)* . . . . profession, occupation
☐ **l'odeur** *(low-dur)* . . . . smell, odor

_____
_____
_____
_____
_____

Maintenant take a deep breath. See if **vous** can fill in the blanks below. **Les réponses correctes sont** at the bottom of **la page.**

1. I speak French. _____

2. He comes from America. _____

3. We learn French. _____

4. They (masc.) have 10 francs. _____

5. She would like a glass of water. _____

6. We need a room. *(chambre)* *Nous avons besoin d'une chambre.*

7. My name is Paul Smith. _____

8 I live in America. _____

9. You are buying a book. _____

10. He orders a beer. _____

In the following Steps, **vous** will be introduced to more **et** more **verbes et** should drill

them in exactly the same way as **vous** did in this section. Look up **les nouveaux mots** *(noo-voh)*

in your **dictionnaire et** make up your own sentences using the same type of pattern. Try
(deek-see-oh-nair)
dictionary

out your **nouveaux mots** for that's how you make them yours to use on your holiday.

Remember, the more **vous** practice **maintenant,** the more enjoyable your trip will be.

Bonne chance!

Be sure to check off your free **mots** in the box provided as **vous apprenez** each one.

RÉPONSES	
1. **Je parle français.**	6. **Nous avons besoin d'une chambre.**
2. **Il vient de l'Amérique.**	7. **Je m'appelle Paul Smith.**
3. **Nous apprenons le français.**	8. **J'habite en Amérique.**
4. **Ils ont dix francs.**	9. **Vous achetez un livre.**
5. **Elle voudrait un verre d'eau.**	10. **Il commande une bière.**

42

(luhr)
L'Heure
hour

Vous know how to tell **les jours de la semaine et les mois de l'année,** so **maintenant**
(lay)
days   week   year

let's learn to tell time. As a **voyageur en France, vous** need to be able to tell time for
(vwhy-ah-zhur)
traveler

réservations, rendez-vous et trains. Voilà les "basics."

What time is it? = **Quelle heure est-il?** *(kel) (uhr) (ay-teel)*	

half past	=	**et demie** _____ *(duh-mee)*
less	=	**moins** *moins* *(mwa(n))*
midnight	=	**minuit** _____ *(mee-nwee)*
noon	=	**midi** _____ *(mee-dee)*

Il est cinq heures. **Il est quatre heures et demie.**

Il est trois heures. **Il est deux heures et demie.**

Il est midi/minuit.

Il est huit heures vingt.

Il est sept heures quarante.   **OU**   **Il est huit heures moins vingt.**

Maintenant fill in the blanks according to **l'heure** indicated **sur l'horloge.**
(luhr)
hour   on   clock

(eel) (ay)
Il est _____.

Il est _____.

Il est _____.

Il est _____.

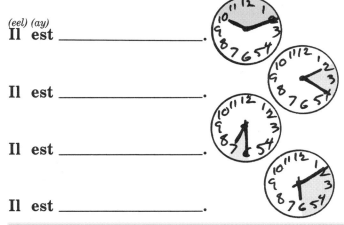

Il est _____.

Il est *quatre heures*

Il est _____.

Il est _____.

RÉPONSES

Il est dix heures dix.
Il est deux heures vingt.
Il est sept heures et demie.
Il est six heures dix.

(Il est cinq heures cinquante.)
Il est six heures moins dix.
Il est midi (ou minuit) vingt.
Il est quatre heures.
Il est une heure et demie.

43

Voilà more time-telling **mots** to add to your **mot** power.

	(kahr)	
un	**quart**	= a quarter
moins le quart		= a quarter to
et quart		= a quarter past

Il est deux heures et quart.   OU   Il est deux heures quinze.

Il est deux heures moins le quart.   OU   Il est une heure quarante-cinq.

Maintenant, your turn.

 Il est *trois heures et quart*.

Il est _____.

 Il est _____.

Il est _____.

Les nombres — see how **importants** they have become! **Maintenant, répondez aux**

questions *(swee-vah⁽ⁿ⁾t)* **suivantes** based on **les horloges** below.
following

Quelle heure est-il?

1. _____

2. *Il est sept heures et demie*

3. _____

4. _____

5. _____

6. _____

7. _____

RÉPONSES

Il est cinq heures quarante-cinq.
7. Il est six heures moins le quart.
6. Il est neuf heures vingt.
5. Il est midi (ou minuit) et quart.

4. Il est une heure et demie.
3. Il est huit heures.
2. Il est sept heures et demie.
1. Il est six heures.

Il est midi (ou minuit) quinze.

44

When **vous** answer a **"Quand"** question, say **"à"** before you give the time.

at

Quand le train arrive-t-il? _à six heures_.

TRAIN
43 6:00

Maintenant, répondez aux questions *(swee-vah⁽ⁿ⁾t)* **suivantes** based on **les horloges** below. Be sure to practice saying each question out loud several times.

(kah⁽ⁿ⁾) *(koh⁽ⁿ⁾-sair)* *(ko-mah⁽ⁿ⁾s-teel)*
Quand le concert commence-t-il? _____.

begins   it

Quand le film commence-t-il? _____.

Quand l'autobus jaune arrive-t-il? _____.

Quand le taxi arrive-t-il? _____.

(oo-vair)
Quand le restaurant est-il ouvert? _à cinq heures_.

open

(fair-may)
Quand le restaurant est-il fermé? _____.

closed

(oh⁽ⁿ⁾) (dee)
A huit heures du matin on dit:

in the   one   says

(mah-dahm)
"Bonjour, Madame Dupont."

Mrs.

A huit heures du soir on dit:

in the

(mad-mwah-zel)
"Bonsoir, Mademoiselle Vartan."

Miss

A une heure de l'après-midi on dit:

(muh-see-uh)
"Bonjour, Monsieur Monet."

Mr.

A dix heures du soir on dit:

"Bonne nuit."

☐ **occupé** *(oh-kew-pay)*.	busy, occupied	_____
— une ligne occupée	engaged telephone line	_____
☐ **officiel** *(oh-fee-see-el)*	official	_____
☐ **l'Orient** *(lor-ee-ah⁽ⁿ⁾)*	Orient	_____
☐ **l'orchestre** *(lor-kess-truh)*	orchestra	_____

45

Remember:

What time is it? = **Quelle heure est-il?**	When/at what time? = **Quand?** **A quelle heure?**

Can **vous** pronounce **et** understand **le**

(pah-rah-grahf) *(swee-vah⁽ⁿ⁾)*
paragraphe suivant?
paragraph

Le train de Lyon arrive à 15:15. Il est

maintenant 15:20. Le train est

(ah⁽ⁿ⁾)(ruh-tar)
en retard. Le train arrive aujourd'hui
late

à 17:15. Demain le train arrive

(ah⁽ⁿ⁾-kor)
encore à 15:15.
again

Voilà more practice exercises. **Répondez aux questions** based on **l'heure** given.

Quelle heure est-il?

1. (10:30) _____
2. (6:30) _____
3. (2:15) *Il est deux heures et quart.*
4. (11:40) _____
5. (12:18) _____
6. (7:20) _____
7. (3:10) _____
8. (4:05) _____
9. (5:35) _____
10. (11:50) _____

☐ **l'omelette** *(low-muh-let)* . . . . omelette _____
☐ **on** *(oh⁽ⁿ⁾)* . . . . one, people, they, we, etc. _____
— **On fait ça.** *(oh⁽ⁿ⁾ fay sah)* . . . . One does that. _____
— **On dit que** . . . *(oh⁽ⁿ⁾ dee kuh)* . . . . They say that . . . _____
46 ☐ **l'optimiste** *(lowp-tee-meest)* . . . . optimist _____

Voilà a quick quiz. Fill in the blanks **avec les nombres corrects. Les réponses sont**
(ah⁽ⁿ⁾) (bah)
en   bas.
below

1. **Une minute a** _____ **secondes.**
   has   (?)

5. **Un mois a** *trente* _____ **jours.**
                         (?)

2. **Une heure a** _____ **minutes.**
                 (?)

6. **Un an a** _____ **mois.**
   year   (?)
   (ah⁽ⁿ⁾)

3. **Un jour a** _____ **heures.**
              (?)

7. **Un an a** _____ **semaines.**
                    (?)

4. **Une semaine a** _____ **jours.**
                   (?)

8. **Un an a** _____ **jours.**
                    (?)

Voilà a sample page from **un horaire de SNCF** — the French national railroad. **Un TEE**
(or-air)   *(ess-n-say-ef)*
timetable
et un rapide (RAP) sont très rapides, un express (EXP) est rapide, et un omnibus (OMN)
              (rah-peed)   fast
est lent.
(lah⁽ⁿ⁾)
slow

Direction Marseille		
Heures	**Trains**	**Destinations**
0:41	50 EXP	Lyon
7:40	19 RAP	Avignon
12:15	10 TEE	Marseille
14:32	4 OMN	St. Raphael
21:40	22 EXP	Lyon

Voilà trois nouveaux verbes pour *(poor)* Step 12.
for

(deer)
dire = to say

(mah⁽ⁿ⁾-zhay)
manger = to eat

(bwahr)
boire = to drink

dire _____ _____

dire

Je	_dis/_	"Bonjour."
Il Elle	_dit/_	"Salut."
Nous	_disons/_	*(noh⁽ⁿ⁾)* "Non." no
Vous	_dites/_	*(wee)* "Oui." yes
Ils Elles	ne _disent/_	*(ree-a⁽ⁿ⁾)* rien. nothing

manger

Je	_mange/_	de la soupe.
Il Elle	_mange/_	un bifteck.
Nous	_mangeons/_	beaucoup.
Vous ne	_mangez/_	*(ree-a⁽ⁿ⁾)* rien. nothing
Ils Elles	_mangent/_	*(ess-kar-go)* des escargots. snails

boire

Je	_bois/_	du lait.
Il Elle	_boit/_	du vin blanc.
Nous	_buvons/_	des bières.
Vous	_buvez/_	un verre d'eau.
Ils Elles	_boivent/_	du thé.

Remember that **"oi"** as in **le verbe "boire"** sounds like "wah." Practice this sound

avec les mots suivants: *(bwah)* **bois**, *(bwah)* **boit**, **trois, soixante, mademoiselle, poivre,** **bonsoir.**
pepper

☐ **ordinaire** *(or-dee-nair)*	ordinary	_____
☐ **organisé** *(or-gah-nee-zay)*	organized	_____
☐ **l'origine** *(loh-ree-zheen)*	origin	_____
— **Je suis d'origine américaine**	I am of American origin.	_____
☐ **l'ouest** *(loo-west)*	west	_____

(tah-blow) **le tableau**	*(bew-row)* **le bureau**	*(wheat)* **8 huit**	*(boh[n]-zhoor)* **bonjour**
(plah-foh[n]) **le plafond**	*(soo-soul)* **le sous-sol**	*(nuf)* **9 neuf**	*(boh[n]-swahr)* **bonsoir**
(kwa[n]) **le coin**	*(gah-rahzh)* **le garage**	*(dees)* **10 dix**	*(bun)* *(nwee)* **bonne nuit**
(fuh-net-ruh) **la fenêtre**	*(low-toe)* **l'auto**	*(blah[n])* **blanc**	*(sah-lew)* **salut**
(lahmp) **la lampe**	*(vwah-tewr)* **la voiture**	*(nwahr)* **noir**	*(ray-free-zhay-rah-tuhr)* **le réfrigérateur**
(lew-mee-air) **la lumière**	*(bee-see-klet)* **la bicyclette**	*(zhown)* **jaune**	*(kwee-zee-nee-air)* **la cuisinière**
(kah-nah-pay) **le canapé**	*(shee-ya[n])* **le chien**	*(roozh)* **rouge**	*(va[n])* **le vin**
(shehz) **la chaise**	*(shah)* **le chat**	*(bluh)* **bleu**	*(bee-air)* **la bière**
(tah-pee) **le tapis**	*(zhar-da[n])* **le jardin**	*(gree)* **gris**	*(lay)* **le lait**
(tahb-luh) **la table**	*(koo-ree-ay)* **le courrier**	*(mah-roh[n])* **marron**	*(buhr)* **le beurre**
(port) **la porte**	*(bwaht) (oh) (let-ruh)* **la boîte aux lettres**	*(vair)* **vert**	*(lah-see-et)* **l'assiette**
(pah[n]-dewl) **la pendule**	*(fluhr)* **les fleurs**	*(rose)* **rose**	*(sell)* **le sel**
(ree-doe) **le rideau**	*(so-net)* **la sonnette**	*(mewl-tee-ko-lor)* **multicolore**	*(pwah-vruh)* **le poivre**
(mewr) **le mur**	*(uh[n])* **1 un**	*(lun-dee)* **lundi**	*(koo-toe)* **le couteau**
(maze-oh[n]) **la maison**	*(duh)* **2 deux**	*(mar-dee)* **mardi**	*(tahs)* **la tasse**
(sahl) (ah)(mah[n]-zhay) **la salle à manger**	*(twah)* **3 trois**	*(mare-kruh-dee)* **mercredi**	*(foor-shet)* **la fourchette**
(lee-veeng-room) **le living-room**	*(kah-truh)* **4 quatre**	*(zhuh-dee)* **jeudi**	*(vair)* **le verre**
(shah[n]-bruh) (ah) (koo-shay) **la chambre à coucher**	*(sank)* **5 cinq**	*(vah[n]-druh-dee)* **vendredi**	*(sair-vee-et)* **la serviette**
(sahl) (duh) (ba[n]) **la salle de bain**	*(sees)* **6 six**	*(sahm-dee)* **samedi**	*(kwee-air)* **la cuiller**
(kwee-zeen) **la cuisine**	*(set)* **7 sept**	*(dee-mah[n]sh)* **dimanche**	*(plah-kar)* **le placard**

STICKY LABELS

This book has over 150 special sticky labels for you to use as you learn new words. When you are introduced to a word, remove the corresponding label from these pages. Be sure to use each of these unique labels by adhering them to a picture, window, lamp, or whatever object it refers to. The sticky labels make learning to speak French much more fun and a lot easier than you ever expected.

For example, when you look in the mirror and see the label, say

(luh)   *(mir-wahr)*
"le miroir."

Don't just say it once, say it again and again.

And once you label the refrigerator, you should never again open that door without saying

(luh)   *(rey-free-zhay-rah-tuhr)*
" le réfrigérateur."

By using the sticky labels, you not only learn new words but friends and family learn along with you!

le pain (pa(n))

le thé (tay)

le café (kah-fay)

le chocolat (show-ko-lah)

l'eau (loh)

le lit (lee)

la couverture (koo-vair-tewr)

l'oreiller (low-ray-yay)

le réveil (ray-vay)

l'armoire (lar-mwahr)

le lavabo (lah-vah-boh)

la douche (doosh)

le W.C. (doo-bul-vay-say)

le miroir (mir-wahr)

le gant de toilette (gah(n)) (duh) (twah-let)

la serviette (sair-vee-et)

la petite serviette (puh-teet) (sair-vee-et)

la serviette de bain (sair-vee-et) (duh) (ba(n))

le crayon (kray-oh(n))

le stylo (stee-low)

le papier (pah-pee-ay)

la lettre (leh-truh)

la carte postale (kart) (pohs-tall)

le timbre-poste (ta(n)-bruh-post)

le livre (lee-vruh)

la revue (ruh-vew)

le journal (zhoor-nahl)

les lunettes (lew-net)

la télévision (tay-lay-vee-zee-oh(n))

la corbeille à papier (kor-bay-uh) (ah) (pah-pee-ay)

le passeport (pass-por)

le billet (bee-ay)

la valise (vah-leez)

le sac à main (sack) (ah) (ma(n))

le portefeuille (port-fuh-yuh)

l'argent (lar-zhah(n))

l'appareil photo (lah-pah-ray) (photo)

la pellicule (peh-lee-kewl)

le maillot (my-oh)

les sandales (sah(n)-dahl)

le savon (sah-voh(n))

la brosse à dents (brohs) (ah)(dah(n))

le dentifrice (dah(n)-tee-frees)

le peigne (pen-yuh)

le manteau (mah(n)-toe)

l'imperméable (la(n)-pear-may-ah-bluh)

le parapluie (pah-rah-plew-ee)

les gants (gah(n))

le chapeau (shah-poh)

les bottes (boat)

les chaussures (show-sewr)

les chaussettes (show-set)

les bas (bah)

le pyjama (pee-zhah-mah)

la chemise de nuit (shuh-meez) (duh) (nwee)

la robe de chambre (rohb) (duh) (shah(n)-bruh)

les pantoufles (pah(n)-too-fluh)

Je suis américain. (zhuh) (swee) (zah-may-ree-ka(n))

Je voudrais apprendre le français (zhuh) (voo-dray) (zah-prah(n)-druh) (luh) (frah(n)-say)

Je m'appelle _____. (zhuh) (mah-pel)

le complet (koh(n)-play)

la cravate (krah-vat)

le mouchoir (moo-shwar)

la chemise (shuh-meez)

le veston (veh-stoh(n))

le pantalon (pah(n)-tah-loh(n))

la robe (rohb)

la blouse (blooz)

la jupe (zhewp)

le chandail (shah(n)-dye)

le soutien-gorge (soo-tee-a(n)-gorzh)

la combinaison (koh(n)-bee-nay-zoh(n))

le slip (sleep)

le tricot de peau (tree-ko) (duh) (poh)

bon appétit (bun) (ah-pay-tee)

occupé (oh-kew-pay)

excusez-moi (ek-skew-zay-mwah)

PLUS . . .

Your book includes a number of other innovative features. At the back of the book, you'll find seven pages of flash cards. Cut them out and flip through them at least once a day.

On pages 112 and 113, you'll find a beverage guide and a menu guide. Don't wait until your trip to use them. Clip out the menu guide and use it tonight at the dinner table. And use the beverage guide to practice ordering your favorite drinks.

By using the special features in this book, you will be speaking French before you know it.

(ah-mew-zay-voo)
Amusez-vous!
have fun

Nord - sud, est - ouest

(nor) north — *(sood)* south — *(est)* east — *(west)* west

If **vous** are looking at **une** *(kart)* **carte et vous** see **les mots suivants,** it should not be too

(dee-fee-seal) **difficile** to figure out what *(map)* *(eel)* **ils** mean. Take an educated guess. **Les réponses sont**

(ah⁽ⁿ⁾)(bah) **en bas.**
difficult / they

(lah-may-reek)(dew)(nor)
l'Amérique du nord

(lah-may-reek)(dew)(sood)
l'Amérique du sud

(lahl-mahn-yuh)(duh)(loo-west)
l'Allemagne de l'ouest

(mare)
la Mer du nord

(lah-freek)
l'Afrique du sud

(lahl-mahn-yuh)(lest)
l'Allemagne de l'est

(leer-lahnd)
l'Irelande du nord

(kah-row-leen)
la Caroline du sud

(tay-ree-twahr)(dew)(nor-west)
les Territoires du nord-ouest

(dah-koh-tah)
le Dakota du nord

(pole)
le Pôle sud

(pole)
le Pôle nord

Les mots français pour north, south, east **et** west **sont** easy to recognize due to their

similarités to **anglais.** So . . .

(nor) **le nord**	=	the north _____
(sood) **le sud**	=	the south *le sud*
(lest) **l'est**	=	the east _____
(loo-west) **l'ouest**	=	the west _____

(dew) **du nord**	=	northern _____
du sud	=	southern _____
(duh) **de l'est**	=	eastern *de l'est*
de l'ouest	=	western _____

These **mots sont très importants.** Learn them **aujourd'hui.** But what about more basic

(dee-rek-see-oh⁽ⁿ⁾) **directions** such as "left," "right," **et** "straight ahead"? Let's learn these **mots.**
directions

(gohsh) **gauche** left

(dwat) **droite** right

straight ahead	=	*(too)(dwah)* **tout droit**
to the left	=	*(ah)(gohsh)* **à gauche**
to the right	=	*(ah)(dwat)* **à droite**

Just as **en anglais,** these **trois mots** go a long way.

(sill) (voo) (play)
s'il vous plaît = please _____

(mare-see)
merci = thank you *merci, merci, merci* _____

(par-doh⁽ⁿ⁾)
pardon = excuse me _____

(ek-skew-zay-mwah)
excusez-moi = excuse me _____

(koh⁽ⁿ⁾vair-sah-see-oh⁽ⁿ⁾) (tee-peek)
Voilà deux conversations typiques pour someone who is trying to find something.
typical

Jean-Paul: **Excusez-moi, mais où est l'Hôtel Cézanne?**
but *(may)*

Claude: **Continuez tout droit, puis tournez à gauche à la deuxième rue et**
continue *(koh⁽ⁿ⁾-tee-new-ay)* turn *(toor-nay)* second *(rew)* street

l'Hôtel est juste à droite.
just *(zhoost)*

Jean-Paul: **Pardon, Monsieur. Où est le Musée français?**

Claude: **Tournez à droite ici, continuez tout droit approximativement cent mètres**

et puis tournez à gauche et le musée est au coin.
(oh) (kwa⁽ⁿ⁾) on the corner

Are you lost? There is no need to be lost if **vous avez** learned the basic **mots de**
(voo) (zah-vay) have

(dee-rek-see-oh⁽ⁿ⁾)
direction. Do not try to memorize these **conversations** because you will never be looking

for precisely these places. One day you might need to ask for **directions** to **"Maxim's"**

ou "le Louvre" ou "l'Hôtel Maurice." Learn the key **mots de direction et** be sure

(day-stee-nah-see-oh⁽ⁿ⁾)
vous can find your **destination.**
destination

What if the person responding to your **question** answers too quickly for you to understand

the entire reply? If so, ask again, saying,

☐ **la paire** *(pair)*	pair	_____
☐ **le pantalon** *(pah⁽ⁿ⁾-tah-loh⁽ⁿ⁾)*	pair of trousers	_____
☐ **le Pape** *(pahp)*	Pope	_____
☐ **parfait** *(par-fay)*	perfect	_____
— **C'est parfait.**	That's fine.	_____

Excusez-moi. Je suis américain et je parle seulement un peu de français. Parlez plus
(suhl-mah(n)) *(puh)* *(plew)*
only a little more

lentement, s'il vous plaît, et répétez votre réponse. Merci beaucoup.
(lah(n)t-mah(n)) *(voh-truh)* *(boh-koo)*
slowly your

Maintenant quand the directions are repeated, **vous** will be able to understand if **vous** *(voo)*
when

avez learned the key **mots** for directions. Quiz yourself by filling in the blanks **en bas** *(zah-vay)*
have

avec les mots corrects en français.

Jean-Louis: **Pardon, Mademoiselle. Où est le restaurant "Le Cygne"?** *(seen-yuh)*
swan

Chantal: **D'ici, continuez** _____, **puis à la troisième** *(dee-see)*
from here   straight ahead   third

_*rue*_____ **tournez à** _____. **Il y a une église. Juste**
street   right   there is

après _____ _____ **encore** _____ *(ah(n)-kor)*
the church   turn   again   right

et le restaurant "Le Cygne" est _____, _*au coin*_.
on the left   on the corner

Bonne chance.

Voilà quatre nouveaux verbes.

(ah-tah(n)-druh)
attendre = to wait for   _attendre, attendre,_

(koh(n)-prah(n)-druh)
comprendre = to understand _____

(vah(n)-druh)
vendre = to sell _____

(ray-pay-tay)
répéter = to repeat _____

☐ **le parc** *(park)* . . . . park   _____
☐ **le parfum** *(par-fuh(n))* . . . . perfume   _____
  — **la parfumerie** *(par-few-muh-ree)* . . . . perfumery   _____
☐ **le parking** *(par-keeng)* . . . . parking lot   _____
☐ **le passeport** *(pass-por)* . . . . passport   _____

51

As always, say each sentence out loud. Say each and every **mot** carefully, pronouncing each French sound as well as **vous** can.

attendre

J' *attends/* _____ le train.

Il *attend/* _____ l'autobus.
Elle
Nous *attendons/* _____ le taxi.

Vous _____ devant l'hôtel.

Ils _____ Jacques.
Elles

vendre

Je *vends/* _____ des fleurs.
_{some}

Il *vend/* _____ du fruit.
Elle

Nous _____ une jaquette.

Vous _____ une banane.

Ils _____ beaucoup de tickets.
Elles

comprendre

Je *comprends/* _____ l'anglais.

Il _____ le français.
Elle
Nous *comprenons/* _____ l'italien.

Vous _____ le menu.

Ils _____ le russe.
Elles

répéter

Je _____ le mot.

Il _____ la réponse.
Elle

Nous _____ les noms.

Vous *répétez/* _____ la leçon.

Ils _____ le verbe.
Elles

Maintenant, see if **vous** can translate the following thoughts **en français.** Les réponses sont en bas.

1. She repeats the word. _____
2. You sell many tickets. _____
3. He waits for the taxi. *Il attend le taxi.*
4. We eat some fruit. _____
5. I speak French. _____
6. I drink a cup of tea. _____

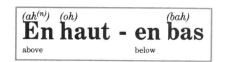

(ah(n)) (oh) (bah)
En haut - en bas
above   below

Step 14

Before **vous commencez** *(koh-mah(n)-say)* Step 14, review Step 8. **Maintenant nous apprenons encore** *(ah(n)-kor)*
begin   more

des mots.

Voilà une maison en France. *(maze-oh(n))*

La chambre à coucher est en haut. *(shah(n)-bruh)* *(koo-shay)*

La salle de bain est aussi en haut. *(sahl)* *(ba(n))*
also

Le bureau est en bas. *(bew-row)*

Le living-room est aussi en bas.

Allez maintenant dans your **chambre à coucher et** look around **la pièce.** *(pea-ess)* Let's learn
(ah-lay)
go

les noms des choses dans la chambre just as **nous avons** learned the various parts of
of the   *(new)* *(zah-voh(n))*

la maison. Be sure to practice saying **les mots** as you write them in the spaces **en bas.**

Also say out loud the example sentences **sous les images.**

le lit *(lee)*	**la couverture** *(koo-vair-teur)* blanket	**l'oreiller** *(low-ray-yay)* pillow
_____	_____	*l'oreiller* _____
J'achète le lit.	**J'ai besoin d'une couverture.** need	**L'oreiller est très grand.**

☐ **la pâtisserie** *(pah-tee-suh-ree)*	pastry, pastry shop	_____
☐ **le peuple français** *(puh-pluh)*	French people	_____
☐ **la pharmacie** *(far-mah-see)*	pharmacy	_____
☐ **la photo** *(pho-toh)*	photo	_____
☐ **la pillule** *(pee-lewl)*	pill	_____

(ray-vay)
le réveil

(lar-mwahr)
l'armoire

Remove the next **cinq** stickers **et** label these **choses dans** your **chambre à coucher.**

_____

J'ai un réveil.

(ee-lee-yah)
Il y a une armoire
there is
dans la chambre.

(oh-bearzh)
La chambre dans un hôtel ou une auberge
youth hostel
(zhuh-ness)
de la jeunesse is for sleeping.

dormir = to sleep. This is **un verbe**

(vwhy-ah-zhur)
important pour le voyageur fatigué.
fatigued

Study **les questions et les réponses**

suivantes based on **l'image à gauche.**

1. **Où est le réveil?**

   Le réveil est sur la table.

2. **Où est la couverture?**

   La couverture est sur le lit.

3. **Où est l'armoire?**

   L'armoire est dans la chambre.

4. **Où est l'oreiller?**

   L'oreiller est sur le lit.

5. **Où est le lit?**

   Le lit est dans la chambre.

6. **Le lit est-il grand ou petit?** *(puh-tee)*
   is it big   small

   Le lit n'est pas grand.
   not

   Le lit est petit.

☐ **le pique-nique** *(peek-neek)* . . . . picnic   _____
☐ **la place** *(plahs)* . . . . place, seat   _____
☐ **le plaisir** *(play-zeer)* . . . . pleasure   _____
   — Avec plaisir. . . . . with pleasure   _____
☐ **la police** *(poh-lees)* . . . . police   _____

Maintenant, vous répondez aux questions based on the previous **image.**

Où est le réveil?   **Où est le lit?**

Le réveil est _____   _____

Let's move into **la salle de bain et** do the same thing.

(lah-vah-boh)
le lavabo

(doosh)
la douche

(doo-bul-vay-say)
le W.C.

le lavabo _____   _____   _____

Il y a un lavabo
there is
dans la salle de bain.

La douche n'est pas

dans la chambre d'hôtel.

Le W.C. n'est pas dans la chambre

d'hôtel. Le W.C. et la douche

(kool-wahr)
sont dans le couloir.
hallway

(mir-wahr)
le miroir _____

(glahs)
la glace _____

(sair-vee-et)
les serviettes *les serviettes* _____
towels

(gah(n)) *(twah-let)*
le gant de toilette _____
wash glove

(puh-teet) (sair-vee-et)
la petite serviette _____

(ba(n))
la serviette de bain _____

(grahnd)
la grande serviette _____
large   towel

Do not forget to remove **les sept** stickers **suivants et** label these **choses dans** your **salle**

de bain.

☐ **la politesse** *(poh-lee-tess)* .... politeness _____
☐ **la politique** *(poh-lee-teek)* .... politics _____
☐ **le port** *(por)* .... port _____
☐ **la Préfecture de Police** *(pray-fek-tewr)* . Police Headquarters _____
☐ **premier** *(pruh-mee-ay)* .... first _____

55

La salle de bain dans une maison en Europe.

baigner = to bathe, so a bathing room

La douche est-elle à droite ou à gauche
  is   it
dans l'image? La douche est

_____.
                    (?)

Où est le W.C. dans l'image? Le W.C. est au milieu, entre _____ et _____.
                                              (oh) (mill-yuh) (ah⁽ⁿ⁾-truh)
                                               in the middle   between   (?)   (?)

Où est le lavabo en haut? Le lavabo est à _____.
                                                                    (?)

Où est le miroir en haut? Le miroir est au-dessus du *lavabo* _____.
                                                                    (?)

Où sont les serviettes dans l'image en haut?

Les serviettes sont au-dessus du_____.   Les serviettes sont sur_____.
                                      (?)   (?)

Remember, **la salle de bain** means a room to bathe in. If **vous êtes dans un restaurant**
                                  (salle) (baigner)   *(et)*
                                                                     are
et vous avez besoin du lavatory, **vous** want to ask for **les cabinets ou les toilettes** *not*
          need   *(kah-bee-nay)*   *(twah-let)*

for **la salle de bain.**

Excusez-moi. Où sont les cabinets?

Restrooms fall **sous** the title of **les toilettes et** they are marked ⬜D⬜ **et** ⬜M⬜. **Vous** will have a sharp surprise if **vous** think the letters stand **pour** "Dudes" **et** "Misses."

⬜D⬜ **représente Dames**   **et** ⬜M⬜ **représente Messieurs.**
       ladies   gentlemen

☐ **le président** *(pray-zee-dah⁽ⁿ⁾)* . . . . president   _____
☐ **la presse** *(press)* . . . . press, media   _____
☐ **le prix** *(pree)* . . . . price, prize   _____
☐ **le problème** *(proh-blem)* . . . . problem   _____
☐ **le programme** *(proh-grahm)* . . . . program   _____

Next stop — **le bureau,** *(bew-row)* specifically **la table ou le bureau dans le**

bureau! Qu'est-ce *(kess)* **qu'il y a sur le bureau?** *(kee-lee-yah)* Let's identify **les choses** which one normally
what   is there

finds **dans le bureau ou** strewn about **la maison.**

(kray-yoh(n))
le crayon

(stee-low)
le stylo

(pah-pee-ay)
le papier

(leh-truh)
la lettre

_____   *le stylo*

(kart) *(pohs-tall)*
la carte postale

(ta(n)-bruh-post)
le timbre-poste

(lee-vruh)
le livre

(ruh-vew) *(mahg-ah-zeen)*
la revue/le magazine

_____   _____   _____   _____

(zhoor-nahl)
le journal

(lew-net)
les lunettes

(tay-lay-vee-zee-oh(n))
la télévision

(kor-bay) *(pah-pee-ay)*
la corbeille à papier

_____   _____   _____   _____

Maintenant, label these **choses dans le bureau avec** your stickers. Do not forget to say

these **mots** out loud whenever **vous les écrivez, vous** see them **ou vous** apply the stickers.
(lay) (zay-kree-vay)
them write

Maintenant, identify **les choses en bas** by filling in each blank **avec le mot correct en**

français.

1

4

5

1. _____

2. _____

6

3. _____

4. _____

2

7

Le Monde

8

5. *le crayon*

6. _____

7. _____

3

L'Express

8. _____

9

10

9. _____

10. _____

Voilà quatre verbes de plus.
(plews)
more

(vwahr)
voir = to see

(ah⁽ⁿ⁾-vwhy-ay)
envoyer = to send

(door-meer)
dormir = to sleep

(troo-vay)
trouver = to find

_____

_____

dormir

_____

Maintenant, fill in the blanks, **à la prochaine page, avec la forme correcte** of these
(pro-shen) *(form)*
on next form

verbes. Practice saying the sentences out loud many times.

☐ **le raisin** *(ray-za⁽ⁿ⁾)*	grape	_____
—**le raisin sec** *(sek)*	raisin (dried grape)	_____
☐ **la recette** *(ruh-set)*	recipe, receipt	_____
☐ **la récréation** *(ray-kray-ah-see-oh⁽ⁿ⁾)*	recreation	_____
☐ **la région** *(ray-zhee-oh⁽ⁿ⁾)*	region, area	

58

58

voir

Je _vois/_ le lit.

Il _voit/_ la couverture.
Elle

Nous _voyons/_ l'hôtel.

Vous _voyez/_ la Tour Eiffel.

Ils _voient/_ la douche.
Elles

envoyer

J' _envoie/_ la lettre.

Il _envoie/_ la carte postale.
Elle

Nous _____ le livre.

Vous _____ quatre cartes postales.

Ils _envoient/_ trois lettres.
Elles

dormir

Je _dors/_ dans la chambre.

Il _dort/_ dans le lit.
Elle

Nous _____ dans l'hôtel.

Vous _____ dans la maison.

Ils _____ sous la couverture.
Elles

trouver

Je _____ le timbre.

Il _trouve/_ les journaux.
Elle

Nous _____ les lunettes.

Vous _____ le Louvre.

Ils _____ les fleurs.
Elles

Remember that **"oi"** sounds like "wah." Practice *(bwah)* **bois**, *(vwah)* **vois**, *(vwah)* **voient**, *(ah$^{(n)}$-vwah)* **envoie** and
drinks see see sends
(ah$^{(n)}$-vwah) **envoient**. Also, **"ent"** at the end of a verb is silent: *(troov)* **trouve** and *(troov)* **trouvent**.
send finds find

The expression *(ness-pah)* **n'est-ce pas** is *(ek-strem-uh-mah$^{(n)}$)* **extrêmement** useful **en français**. Added onto a sentence,
extremely

it turns the sentence into a question for which **la réponse** is usually **"oui."** It has only one

form and is much simpler than **en anglais**.

C'est un livre, n'est-ce pas? *(ness-pah)*	=	It's a book, isn't it?
Jacqueline est belle, n'est-ce pas?	=	Jacqueline is beautiful, isn't she?
Vous êtes français, n'est-ce pas?	=	You're French, aren't you?

Step 15

$$\boxed{\begin{array}{c}\textit{(koo-ree-ay)}\\ \textbf{Le Courrier}\\ \text{mail}\end{array}}$$

Vous know **maintenant** how to count, how to ask **questions,** how to use **verbes avec** the

"plug-in" formula, how to make statements, **et** how to describe something, be it the

location of **un hôtel ou la couleur d'une maison.** Let's now take the basics that **vous avez**

$\qquad$ *(dewn)* of a $\qquad$ *(voo) (zah-vay)*

learned **et** expand them in special areas that will be most helpful in your travels. What

does everyone do on a holiday? Send postcards, **n'est-ce-pas?** Let's learn exactly how **le**

$\qquad$ *(ness-pah)*

(bew-row) $\quad$ *(post)*
bureau de poste français (P et T) works.
post office

le courrier . . .

en Amérique

en Espagne

en Angleterre

en Italie

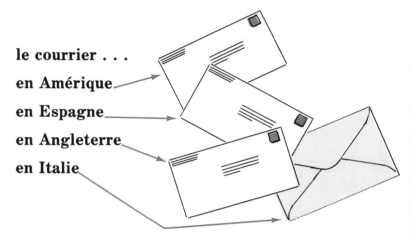

(lay) *(pay-ay-tay)*
Les P et T (Poste et Télécommunications) is where you need to go **en France** to buy
post office

a stamp, mail a package, send a telegram or use the telephone. **Voilà** some **mots**

(nay-say-sair)
nécessaires pour le bureau de poste.
necessary

la lettre	**la carte postale**	*(ta(n)-bruh-pohst)* **le timbre-poste**	*(tay-lay-grahm)* **le télégramme**

la lettre _____ _____ _____

☐ **la résidence** *(ray-zee-dah(n)s)* . . . . residence _____
☐ **la résistance** *(ray-zee-stah(n)s)* . . . . resistance _____
☐ **la révolution** *(ray-voh-lew-see-oh(n))* . . . . . revolution _____
$\quad$ **— 1789 - la Révolution française** . . . . . French Revolution _____
60 ☐ **la route** *(root)* . . . . route, highway _____

(pah-kay) *(koh-lee)*
le paquet/le colis

(bwaht) *(oh)* *(let-ruh)*
la boîte aux lettres

(par) *(ah-vee-oh*(n)*)*
par avion

(ge-shay)
le guichet
window/counter

par avion

(kah-bean) *(tay-lay-phone-eek)*
la cabine téléphonique

(tay-lay-phone)
le téléphone

(pay-ay-tay) *(bew-row)*
les P et T/le bureau de poste

Les P et T en France *(oh*(n)*)* *(too)* ont tout. Vous *(ah*(n)*-vwhy-ay)* envoyez les télégrammes, les lettres et les cartes
has   everything   send

postales *(dew)* du bureau de poste.   Vous achetez les timbres dans le bureau de poste.
from the

(tay-lay-phone-ay)
Vous téléphonez du bureau de poste.   Le bureau de poste est *(zhay-nay-rahl-mah*(n)*)* généralement open from
telephone   generally

8:00 du matin à 7:00 du soir weekdays et 8:00 à 12:00 le *(sahm-dee)* samedi.   If vous avez besoin
Saturday   need

to call home **en Amérique,** this can be done **au bureau de poste et** is called **un** *(ah-pel)* **appel**
at the   call

(a(n)*-tair-ewr-ba*(n)*)*
interurbain.   Okay.   First step — **entrez dans** les P et T.
long distance

The following **est une** *(bun)* **bonne** sample **conversation.**   Familiarize yourself **avec** *(say)* **ces mots**
these

maintenant.

GUICHET 7

Excusez-moi.
Où achète-t-on
des timbres?

Au guichet
numéro 7.

☐ **le sac** *(sack)* . . . .   sack   _____
☐ **sacré** *(sah-kray)* . . . .   sacred   _____
  —**Sacré-Coeur à Paris** *(sah-kray kur)* . . .   Sacred Heart in Paris   _____
☐ **sage** *(sahzh)* . . . .   wise, well-behaved   _____
☐ **la saison** *(say-zoh*(n)*)* . . . .   season   _____

Je voudrais des timbres pour deux lettres pour l'Amérique et aussi des timbres pour deux cartes postales pour l'Amérique.

Par avion?

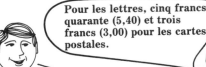 Pour les lettres, cinq francs quarante (5,40) et trois francs (3,00) pour les cartes postales.

Combien est-ce que ça coûte?

 Oui, par avion, s'il vous plaît. Je voudrais aussi des timbres pour deux lettres pour la France. Combien est-ce?

Un franc soixante (1,60).

Bon.

Voilà les timbres. Ça fait dix francs (10F).

Merci bien, Madame.

Next step — **vous** ask **questions** like those **en bas** depending upon what **vous voudriez.** *(voo-dree-ay)* _{want}

Où est-ce qu'on achète des timbres?
(ess) *(koh⁽ⁿ⁾)* *(nah-shet)*
_{one} _{buy}

Où est-ce qu'on envoie un télégramme?
(ess) *(koh⁽ⁿ⁾)* *(nah⁽ⁿ⁾-vwah)*

Où est-ce qu'on achète une carte postale?

Où est-ce qu'on envoie un paquet?

Où est-ce qu'on téléphone?

Où est la cabine téléphonique? *(ay)*

Où est-ce qu'on fait un appel interurbain?
(ah-pel) *(a⁽ⁿ⁾-tair-ewr-ba⁽ⁿ⁾)*
_{call} _{long distance}

Combien est-ce que ça coûte?

Où est-ce qu'on fait un appel local?
(low-kahl)

Où est la boîte aux lettres?

Répétez many times **ces phrases en haut.** *(say)* *(frahz)*
_{these} _{sentences}

Maintenant, quiz yourself. See if **vous** can translate the following thoughts **en français.**

Les réponses sont en bas de la prochaine page. *(pro-shen)*
_{next}

1. Where is the telephone booth? _____

2. Where does one make a phone call? _____

3. Where does one make a local phone call? _____

4. Where does one make a long-distance phone call?_____

5. Where is the post office? _____

☐ **la salutation** *(sah-lew-tah-see-oh⁽ⁿ⁾)* ..... greeting _____
☐ **le sandwich** *(sah⁽ⁿ⁾-dweech)* .... sandwich _____
☐ **la sauce** *(sohs)* .... sauce _____
☐ **le saumon** *(soh-moh⁽ⁿ⁾)* .... salmon _____
☐ **la science** *(see-ah⁽ⁿ⁾s)* .... science _____

6. Where does one buy stamps? _____

7. How much is it? _____

8. Where does one send a package? _____

9. Where does one send a telegram? _____

10. Where is window eight? _____

Voilà quatre nouveaux verbes.

(fare)
faire = to do/make   *(moh⁽ⁿ⁾-tray)* **montrer** = to show   *(ay-kreer)* **écrire** = to write   *(pay-yay)* **payer** = to pay

_____   _____   *écrire*   _____

faire

Je *fais/* _____ **un appel.**

Il
Elle *fait/* _____ **le lit.** *(lee)* bed

Nous *faisons/* _____ **beaucoup.** a lot

Vous ne *faites/* _____ **rien.** *(ree-a⁽ⁿ⁾)* nothing

Ils
Elles *font/* _____ **tout.** *(too)* everything

montrer

Je *montre/* _____ **le livre.**

Il   **vous**
Elle to you _____ **le bureau.**

Nous **vous** _____ **le château.** to you   castle

Vous **me** _____ **la lettre.** *(muh)* to me

Ils   **me**
Elles to me _____ **les P et T.**

écrire

J' *écris/* _____ **une lettre.**

Il
Elle *écrit/* _____ **beaucoup.**

Nous *écrivons/* _____ **un télégramme.**

Vous *écrivez/* _____ **votre signature.** *(voh-truh)(seen-yah-tewr)* your   signature

Ils   n'
Elles *écrivent/* _____ **rien.**

payer

Je *paie/* _____ **l'addition.** *(lah-dee-see-oh⁽ⁿ⁾)* bill in restaurant

Il
Elle *paie/* _____ **la taxe.** tax

Nous *payons/* _____ **la note.** bill in hotel

Vous _____ **le prix.** *(pree)* price

Ils   ne
Elles *paient/* _____ **rien.**

63

Step 16

(ko-mah⁽ⁿ⁾) *(pay-yay)*
Comment payer
how to pay

Oui, il y a aussi bills to pay **en France. Vous** have just finished your **repas délicieux** *(ruh-pah)(day-lee-see-yuh)*
there are also meal delicious

et vous voudriez l'addition et vous voudriez payer. Que faites-vous? Vous call for *(fet)*
bill do you do

(sair-vur) *(gar-soh⁽ⁿ⁾)* *(sair-vuz)*
le serveur (le garçon) ou la serveuse.
waiter waitress

> Excusez-moi. Je voudrais l'addition, s'il vous plaît.

> Bien sûr, Monsieur. Une minute.

Le serveur will normally reel off what **vous** *(voo)*

(zah-vay)
avez eaten, while writing rapidly. **Il** will then

place **une petite feuille de papier sur la** *(puh-teet) (fuh-yuh)*
little sheet

table that looks like **l'addition dans l'image,**

while saying something like:

(fay) *(muh-see-uh)*
"Ça fait vingt-six francs soixante, Monsieur."
makes

Vous will pay **le serveur** or perhaps **vous** will pay **à la caisse.** *(kess)* Tipping **en France est**
at cashier

généralement much easier than **en Amérique.** If your bill or the menu is marked

(sair-vees) *(koh⁽ⁿ⁾-pree)*
"Service compris," then your tip has already been included in your bill. If not, then a
service included

> Excellent dîner. Merci.

> Il n'y a pas de quoi. *(eel-nee-ah)(pah) (kwah)*
> you're welcome
> Au revoir, Monsieur.

15% tip left **sur la table** is customary. Most

French eating establishments are **"Service**

compris," but don't forget to look. You

might find some that are **"Service non** not

compris."

☐ **second** *(suh-goh⁽ⁿ⁾)* .... second _____
☐ **le/la secrétaire** *(suh-kray-tair)* .... secretary _____
☐ **la sécurité** *(say-kew-ree-tay)* .... security _____
☐ **le sentiment** *(sah⁽ⁿ⁾-tee-mah⁽ⁿ⁾)* .... feeling _____
64 ☐ **la situation** *(see-tew-ah-see-oh⁽ⁿ⁾)* .... situation _____

Remember these key **mots** when dining out **à la française.** *(frah⁽ⁿ⁾-sez)*

in the French manner

(muh-new) **le menu** or **la carte** *(kart)*	*(poor-bwahr)* **le pourboire** tip
(lah-dee-see-oh⁽ⁿ⁾) **l'addition**	**service compris**

La politesse est très importante en France. You will feel more **français** if you practice
(poh-lee-tess)
politeness

and use **ces expressions.** *(say)* *(zek-spreh-see-oh⁽ⁿ⁾)*
these expressions

excusez-moi or **pardon**

s'il vous plaît

merci beaucoup or **merci bien** *(boh-koo)* *(bee-a⁽ⁿ⁾)*

il n'y a pas de quoi *(eel) (nee-ah) (pah) (duh) (kwah)*
you're welcome/it's nothing

Voilà une sample **conversation** involving paying **la note** when leaving **un hôtel.** *(note)*
bill

Jeannette:	**Excusez-moi, Monsieur. Voudriez-vous me préparer la note?** *(voo-dree-ay-voo)* *(muh)(pray-pah-ray)* would you for me prepare
L'Hôtelier:	**Quelle chambre, s'il vous plaît?** *(low-tell-ee-ay)* *(kel)* hotelkeeper what
Jeannette:	**Numéro trois cent dix.**
L'Hôtelier:	**Merci. Une minute, s'il vous plaît.**
L'Hôtelier:	**Voilà la note. Ça fait quatre-vingt-dix francs vingt.**
Jeannette:	**Merci beaucoup (et Jeannette** hands him **un billet de cent francs.** **L'Hôtelier** returns shortly **et dit)** *(dee)* says
L'Hôtelier:	**Voilà votre reçu et votre monnaie (9F,8). Merci et au revoir.** *(voh-truh)(ruh-sue)* *(oh) (ruh-vwahr)* your receipt money goodbye

Simple, right? If **vous avez** any **problème avec les nombres,** just ask the person to write

out **la somme** so that **vous** can be sure you understand everything correctly. *(sohm)*
sum

"S'il vous plaît, écrivez-moi la somme. Merci." *(ay-kree-vay-mwah)*
write for me sum

Let's take a break from **l'argent et,** starting **à la prochaine page,** learn some **nouveaux**

fun **mots.**

- ☐ **le ski** *(ski)* . . . . skiing _____
- — **le ski-nautique** *(ski-no-teek)* . . . . water skiing _____
- ☐ **la Sorbonne** *(sore-bun)* . . . . part of University of Paris _____
- ☐ **la soupe** *(soup)* . . . . soup _____
- ☐ **le spectacle** *(spek-tah-kluh)* . . . . spectacle, performance _____

Il est <u>en bonne forme</u>.

Il est <u>malade</u>.
(mah-lahd)
sick

(boh⁽ⁿ⁾)
C'est <u>bon</u>.
good

(suh) (nay) (pah) (boh⁽ⁿ⁾)
Ce n'est pas bon.
not

(mow-vay)
C'est <u>mauvais</u>.
bad

(showd)
L'eau est <u>chaude</u>.
warm

Elle a 50 degrés.
has

(fwahd)
L'eau est <u>froide</u>.
cold

Elle a 17 degrés.

(for)
Vous parlez <u>fort</u>.
loudly

(deuce-mah⁽ⁿ⁾)
Nous parlons <u>doucement</u>.
softly

(koort)
La ligne rouge est <u>courte</u>.

(lohng)
La ligne bleue est <u>longue</u>.

La femme est <u>grande</u>.

L'enfant est <u>petite</u>.

(grow)
Le livre rouge est <u>gros</u>.
thick

(ma⁽ⁿ⁾s)
Le livre vert est <u>mince</u>.
thin

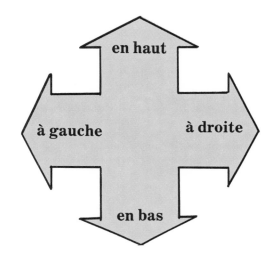

en haut

à gauche

à droite

en bas

(ah) (luhr)
20 kilomètres à l'heure
per hour

200 kilomètres à l'heure

(lah⁽ⁿ⁾)
<u>lent</u>
slow

(veet) (rah-peed)
<u>vite/rapide</u>
fast

☐ **le sport** *(spor)* . . . . sport
☐ **stopper** *(stow-pay)* . . . . to stop
☐ **stupide** *(stew-peed)* . . . . stupid
☐ **la Suède** *(sue-ed)* . . . . Sweden
☐ **la Suisse** *(swees)* . . . . Switzerland

Les montagnes sont hautes. *(moh(n)-tan-yuh)* *(oht)* Elles ont 2000 mètres de haut. *(meh-truh)*
mountains   high   have   meters

Les montagnes sont basses. *(bahs)* Elles sont seulement 800
low

mètres de haut.

Le grand-père est **vieux.** *(vee-yuh)* Il a soixante-dix **ans.** *(ah(n))*
old   has   years

L'enfant est **jeune.** *(zhun)* Il a seulement dix ans.
young

La chambre d'hôtel est **chère.** *(share)* Elle coûte 94,50 F.
expensive

La chambre de l'AJ est **bon marché.** *(lah-zhee)* *(boh(n))(mar-shay)* Elle coûte 30,50 F.
youth hostel   inexpensive

J'ai 2.000 F. Je suis **riche.** *(reesh)* C'est **beaucoup** d'argent. *(boh-koo)*
rich   a lot

Il a seulement 4F. Il est **pauvre.** *(poh-vruh)* C'est **peu** d'argent. *(puh)*
poor   little

Voilà de nouveaux verbes.
some

(sah-vwahr)	*(poo-vwahr)*	*(duh-vwahr)*	*(leer)*
savoir = to know (a fact, an address, etc.)	**pouvoir** = to be able to/can	**devoir** = to have to/ must/to owe	**lire** = to read

_____   _____   *devoir*   _____

Les verbes "savoir," "pouvoir" et "devoir," along with **le verbe "vouloir,"** can be joined

with another **verbe:**

nous savons trouver l'adresse	**nous pouvons parler**	**nous devons payer**
know how to find	can speak	must pay
nous savons parler français	**nous pouvons comprendre**	**nous devons manger**
	understand	eat

☐ **supérieur** *(sue-pay-ree-ur)*	....	superior, upper	_____
☐ **le surprise** *(sewr-preez)*	....	surprise	_____
☐ **sympathique** *(sa(n)-pah-teek)*	....	likeable, nice	_____
— **Qu'il est sympa!** *(kee-lay)*	....	Oh, he's so nice.	_____
☐ **le système** *(see-stem)*	....	system	_____

Study their pattern closely as **vous** will use **beaucoup de ces verbes.**
_{a lot} _(say) _{these}

savoir

Je _sais/_ tout.
_{everything}

Il _sait/_ l'adresse.
Elle

Nous _savons/_ parler français.

Vous _____ commander une bière.

Ils ne _savent/_ pas l'adresse.
Elles_{do not}

pouvoir

Je _peux/_ parler français.

Il _peut/_ comprendre l'anglais.
Elle

Nous _pouvons/_ boire.

Vous _pouvez/_ entrer.

Ils _peuvent/_ parler français aussi.
Elles

devoir

Je _dois/_ payer la note.

Il _doit/_ rester à l'hôtel.
Elle

Nous _devons/_ visiter Paris.

Vous nous _devez/_ 5 francs.
_{to us}

Ils _doivent/_ payer l'addition.
Elles

lire

Je _lis/_ le livre.

Il _lit/_ le journal.
Elle

Nous _lisons/_ le menu.

Vous _lisez/_ beaucoup.

Ils _lisent/_ tout.
Elles

Pouvez-vous translate these thoughts **en bas en français? Les réponses sont en bas.**

1. I can speak French. _____

2. He must pay now. _____

3. We don't know the address. _____

4. You owe us ten francs. _Vous nous devez dix francs._

5. She knows everything. _____

6. I am able to speak a little French. _____

En France, il y a trois main **repas** *(ruh-pah)* to enjoy every day, plus **un café et** perhaps **une**
(eel-ee-ah)
meals

(pah-tee-suh-ree)
pâtisserie pour le voyageur fatigué late in **l'après-midi.**
pastry

(puh-tee)(day-zhuh-nay) **le petit déjeuner**	=	breakfast . . . this is a "continental breakfast," with **café ou thé et** toast **ou croissant.** Be sure to check serving times before retiring.
(day-zhuh-nay) **le déjeuner**	=	lunch . . . . . . generally served from 12:00 to 14:00. You will be able to find any type of meal, **grand ou petit,** served at this time.
(dee-nay) **le dîner**	=	dinner . . . . . generally served from 19:30 to 22:00, **les Français** eat much later than Americans. This meal is meant to be relished, surrounded by good friends and a pleasant atmosphere.

If **vous** look around you **dans un restaurant français, vous** will see that some **coutumes**
(koo-tewm)
customs

françaises sont différentes from ours. **Le pain** may be set directly on the tablecloth,
(dee-fay-rah$^{(n)}$t)   *(pa$^{(n)}$)*
bread

elbows are often rested **sur la table** and please do not forget to mop up your **sauce avec**

votre pain! **Vous** will hear **"Bon Appétit"** before **votre repas et** an inquiring **"C'était**
(bun) (ah-pay-tee)   *(say-tay)*

bon?" after **vous** have finished. **Le serveur** is asking if **vous** enjoyed **votre repas et** if it

tasted good. A smile **et** a **"Oui, merci"** will tell him that you enjoyed it.

Maintenant, it may be **petit déjeuner** time **à Denver, mais vous êtes en France et il est**
(may)
but

19:00. Most **restaurants français** post **le menu** outside. Always read it before

entering so **vous savez** what type of **repas et prix vous** will encounter inside. Most
(pree)
prices

restaurants offer **un plat du jour ou un menu à prix fixe.** This is a complete **repas**
(plah) (dew)
special meal of the day   fixed

at a fair **prix.** In addition, **il y a** all the following main categories **sur le menu.**
(muh-new)

□ **le village** *(vee-lahzh)* . . . . village   _____
□ **le vin** *(va$^{(n)}$)* . . . . wine   _____
□ **la visite** *(vee-zeet)* . . . . visit   _____
□ **la vitamine** *(vee-tah-mean)* . . . . vitamin   _____
□ **le vocabulaire** *(voh-kah-bew-lair)* . . . . . . vocabulary   _____

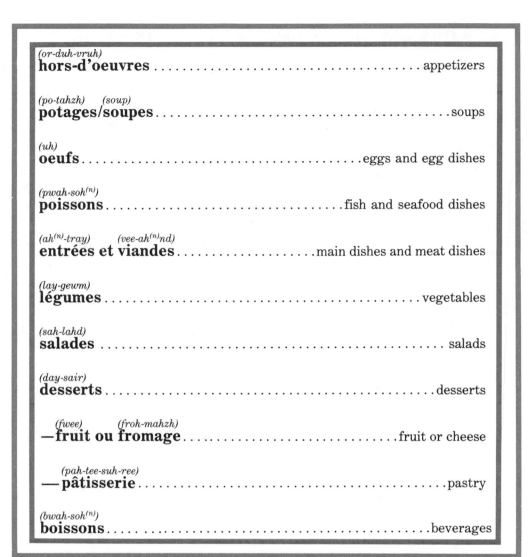

(or-duh-vruh)
hors-d'oeuvres . . . . appetizers

(po-tahzh) *(soup)*
potages/soupes . . . . soups

(uh)
oeufs . . . . eggs and egg dishes

(pwah-soh⁽ⁿ⁾)
poissons . . . . fish and seafood dishes

(ah⁽ⁿ⁾-tray) *(vee-ah⁽ⁿ⁾nd)*
entrées et viandes . . . . main dishes and meat dishes

(lay-gewm)
légumes . . . . vegetables

(sah-lahd)
salades . . . . salads

(day-sair)
desserts . . . . desserts

(fwee) *(froh-mahzh)*
—fruit ou fromage . . . . fruit or cheese

(pah-tee-suh-ree)
— pâtisserie . . . . pastry

(bwah-soh⁽ⁿ⁾)
boissons . . . . beverages

Most **restaurants** also offer **les specialtiés de la maison ou** special meals prepared **par** *(pahr)* by *(spay-see-ah-lee-tay)*

le chef. *(shef)* And if **vous** are sampling the wine, don't forget to ask about the **vin de la maison.** house wine

Maintenant for a preview of delights to come . . . At the back of this **livre vous trouvez** *(troo-vay)*

a sample **menu français. Lisez le menu aujourd'hui et apprenez les nouveaux mots!**

Quand vous are ready to leave for **Europe,** cut out **le menu,** fold it **et** carry it in your

pocket, wallet **ou** purse. **Vous pouvez aller dans** any **restaurant et** feel prepared. (May *(poo-vay)* can *(zah-lay)*

I suggest studying **le menu** after, **et** not before, **vous avez** eaten!)

Most "w" words are foreign additions to **le français.**
- ☐ **le wagon** *(vah-goh⁽ⁿ⁾)* . . . . railroad car   _____
- ☐ **le week-end** *(week-end)* . . . . weekend   _____
- ☐ **le western** *(wes-tairn)* . . . . western (film)   _____
- ☐ **le whisky** *(we-skee)* . . . . whisky   _____

In addition, learning the following should help you to identify what kind of meat **ou** poultry

vous commandez et comment it will be prepared.

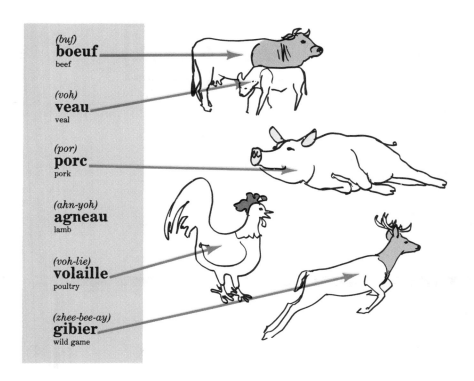

(buf)
boeuf
beef

(voh)
veau
veal

(por)
porc
pork

(ahn-yoh)
agneau
lamb

(voh-lie)
volaille
poultry

(zhee-bee-ay)
gibier
wild game

(kwee)
cuit = cooked

(roh-tee)
rôti = roasted

(free)
frit = fried

(kwee) (toh) (foor)
cuit au four = baked

(gree-ay)
grillé = grilled

(far-see)
farci = stuffed

(lay-gewm)
Vous will also get **légumes avec votre repas et** perhaps **une salade verte,** after **l'entrée.**
vegetables   *(vairt)*
                                                                              green

(mar-shay)
One day at an open-air **marché** will teach you **les noms** for all the different kinds of
market

(fwee)
légumes et fruits, plus it will be a delightful experience for you. **Vous pouvez** always
                                                                        can

(voo) (zoo-blee-ay)
consult your menu guide at the back of **ce livre** if **vous oubliez le nom correct.**
                                                              forget

(voo-dree-ay)
Maintenant vous avez decided what **vous voudriez manger et le serveur arrive.**

Et comme boisson?

Je voudrais la soupe du jour
et une côtelette de porc.

Un verre de vin blanc,
s'il vous plaît.

☐ **le zèbre** *(zeh-bruh)* . . . . zebra _____
— **zébré** *(zay-bray)* . . . . striped _____
☐ **le zèle** *(zel)* . . . . zeal, ardor _____
— **zélé** *(zay-lay)* . . . . zealous _____
☐ **le zénith** *(zay-neat)* . . . . zenith, peak _____

N'oubliez pas *(noo-blee-ay)* *(pah)* to treat yourself to **un dessert français.** You would not want to miss out on
don't forget

trying **les desserts suivants.**

---

une crème caramel *(krem)* *(kah-rah-mel)*
custard with burnt sugar sauce

une tarte aux pommes *(tart)* *(oh)* *(pohm)*
apple pie

une mousse au chocolat *(moose)* *(oh)* *(show-ko-lah)*
whipped chocolate pudding

des ananas *(day)* *(zah-nah-nah)* **au rhum** *(oh)* *(rome)*
pineapple   in rum

After completing **votre repas,** call **le serveur et** pay just as **vous avez** already learned in

Step 16:

> **Monsieur, je voudrais l'addition, s'il vous plaît.**

En bas il y a une sample **carte** to help you prepare for your holiday.

RESTAURANT RELAIS DE POSTE

LA CARTE

HORS-D'OEUVRE

Oeufs durs mayonnaise (hard-boiled eggs with mayonnaise)	6,50 F
Salade de tomates (sliced tomatoes)	6,50
Salade niçoise (mixed salad with tuna, green beans and potatoes) .	8,00
Filets d'anchois (anchovies)	8,00
Artichaut vinaigrette (artichoke with oil and vinegar sauce)	10,50

POTAGES

Soupe à l'oignon (French onion soup)	8,00
Potage aux asperges (creamed asparagus)	9,50
Bouillabaisse (fish soup)	12,00
Bisque de homard (lobster bisque)	12,00

POISSONS ET FRUITS DE MER

Huîtres (oysters)	32,00
Coquille St. Jacques (scallops)	25,00
Langoustines mayonnaise (boiled lobster with mayonnaise)	35,00
Moules (mussels)	30,00
Sole meunière (fried sole in butter)	28,50

ENTRÉES ET VIANDES

Escalope de veau à la crème (veal cutlets in cream sauce)	50,00
Tournedos bearnaise (beef tenderloin in bearnaise sauce)	50,00
Côtes d'agneau grillé (grilled lamb chops)	38,00
Daube de boeuf (marinated beef pot roast)	40,00
Canard au poivre vert (duck with green peppers)	45,00

Poulet à l'estragon (tarragon chicken)	40,00
Tripes (stomach lining of calf or beef)	35,00

LÉGUMES

Gratin dauphinois (scalloped potatoes)	8,00
Légumes de saison (seasonal vegetables)	9,00
Champignons sautés provençal (sauted mushrooms)	10,50
Salade verte (tossed green salad)	8,00

FROMAGE

Plateau de fromage, par personne (cheese selection)	15,00

DESSERTS

Pâtisserie (pastry from tray)	8,50
Glace à la fraise (strawberry ice cream)	6,50
Corbeille de fruits (choice of fruit)	6,00
Crèpes Suzette (crèpes with liqueur)	15,00
Pêche Melba (peach and vanilla ice cream)	8,50

BOISSONS

Vin (verre)	6,00
Vin (carafe)	15,00
Bière	6,00
Eau minérale (mineral water)	2,50
Limonade	3,00
Jus de fruit (fruit juice)	4,00
Lait	3,00
Café	2,50
Thé	2,50

Service 15% compris

☐ **le zéphyr** *(zay-feer)*	balmy breeze	_____
☐ **zéro** *(zay-row)*	zero	_____
☐ **le zodiaque** *(zoh-dee-ak)*	zodiac	_____
— **Je suis de signe "poisson."**	I am a "pisces."	_____
☐ **la zoologie** *(zoh-oh-loh-zhee)*	zoology	_____

Le petit déjeuner est un peu différent (dee-fay-rah(n)) [little] because it is fairly standardized **et vous** will frequently take it at **votre hôtel** as **il est généralment** included in **le prix de votre chambre**. **En bas il y a** a sample of what **vous pouvez** expect to greet you **le matin**.

Petit déjeuner - Simple .....6F (sa(n)-pluh)

café au lait
coffee and steamed milk
pain

Petit déjeuner - Complet ...12F (koh(n)-play)

café au lait

croissants

beurre et confiture
jam

Petit déjeuner à l'anglaise
in the English manner

(these additions usually only available in large hotels catering to foreigners)

jus d'orange

jus de pamplemousse
grapefruit

jambon
ham

saucisse
sausage

oeuf à la coque
egg   soft-boiled

oeuf mollet
medium-boiled.

oeufs brouillés
scrambled

omelette nature

Des phrases pratiques

Combien coûte le petit déjeuner?

Je voudrais deux complets, s'il vous plaît.

Je voudrais des croissants et du thé, s'il vous plaît.

Veuillez faire monter le petit déjeuner à la chambre dix, (vuh-yay) (fare)
please   have   brought up

s'il vous plaît.

83

Step 19

(*kess*) (*key*)
Qu'est-ce qui est différent about **le téléphone en France?** Well, **vous** never notice such
what

things until **vous** want to use them. Be warned **maintenant** that **téléphones en France**

are much less numerous than **en Amérique.** Nevertheless, **le téléphone** allows you to

(*veel*)
reserve **les chambres d'hôtel dans** another **ville,** call friends, **demander des renseigne-**
city

ments sur les billets de théâtre, de concert ou de ballet, make emergency calls, check

(*mew-zay*)
on the hours of a **musée,** rent **une automobile et** all those other **choses** which **nous faisons**
museum

(*lee-bear-tay*)
on a daily basis. It also gives you a certain amount of **liberté quand vous pouvez** make

(*ah-pel*)
your own **appels de téléphone.**
calls

Having **un téléphone dans votre maison n'est pas** as common **en France** as **en Amérique.**
is   not

That means that **vous devez savoir où trouver les téléphones:** in the **bureaux de poste,**
must   to find   post offices

on the street, in the **cafés** and in the lobby of **votre hôtel.** Often **vous devez acheter**

(*zhuh-toh*$^{(n)}$)
a token, called **un jeton,** before you use a public **téléphone.**

Voilà un téléphone public français.

So far, so good. **Maintenant,** let's read the
instructions for using **le téléphone.** This **est**
one of those moments when you realize,

(*nuh*) (*swee*) (*pah*) (*zah*$^{(n)}$)
Je ne suis pas en Amérique.
am   not

So let's learn how to operate **le téléphone.**

If **vous** use **le téléphone dans un bar ou un café,** be sure to ask, "**Est-ce qu'un jeton** *(ess)* *(kuh⁽ⁿ⁾)* *(zhuh-toh⁽ⁿ⁾)*

(nay-say-sair)
est nécessaire?" The **bar** employee will sell you **un jeton** to use if it is needed **et,** if not, then **vous pouvez** use regular **pièces de monnaie.**

Consultez le tableau des taxes ci-contre et préparez votre monnaie en fonction du
indicator   of   prices   attached   prepare   depending upon

temps pendant lequel vous désirez parler, car l'appareil ne rend pas la monnaie.
time   during   which   desire   for   does not return

Décrochez le combiné et composez le numéro
lift   receiver   dial

Vous ne pourrez introduire les pièces qu'après la réponse de votre correspondant.
insert   coins   only after   party

Lorsque le demandé a répondu, la tonalité d'appel se transforme en une tonalité
when   called party   has answered   dial tone   changes   to   tone

de paiement (bip-bip-bip . . .)
payment

Introduisez immediatement les pièces.
insert

La tonalité de paiement ne s'arrête et vous ne pouvez parler que lorsque
stops   only   when

l'appareil a encaissé une somme suffisante.
has registered   sum

Pour prolonger la conversation introduisez d'autres pièces,
to   lengthen   additional

—à n'importe quel moment durant la conversation
at any time   during

—très rapidement, dès que vous reentendez la tonalité de paiement (bip-bip-bip)
quickly   as soon as   hear again

Anglais	Français	Anglais	Français
telephone	= **le téléphone**	to telephone = **téléphoner**	
		= **faire un appel**	
telephone booth	= **la cabine téléphonique**		
		operator	= **le téléphoniste**
telephone book	= *(lah-new-air)* **l'annuaire**		= **le standardiste**
telephone conversation	= **la conversation téléphonique**	token	= **le jeton**

So **maintenant vous savez comment faire un appel en France.** **Vous** will find that **la**

(ma-zhoh-ree-tay) *(day)* *(new-may-row)*
majorité **des numéros en France sont six** digits, such as **47-06-14.** However, **à Paris,**

il y a sept digits, such as **326-69-12. Il y a aussi** area codes, or *(a⁽ⁿ⁾-dee-ka-teef)* *(ray-zhee-oh-noh)* **indicatifs régionaux,**
there are

and these are listed in *(lah-new-air)* **l'annuaire.** **Les téléphones dans les maisons** also have an added
telephone book

feature different from ours in that they come equipped with an extra listening device as

extension phones are rare.

When answering **le téléphone, vous** pick up **le récepteur et** say, *(ray-sep-tur)*
receiver

"**Allô? C'est** _____ *(ah)(lah-pah-ray)* **à l'appareil.**"
votre nom on the phone

When saying good-bye, **vous dites,** *(ah)(duh-ma⁽ⁿ⁾)* "**A demain**" **ou** *(oh)* *(ruh-vwahr)* "**Au revoir.**" **Voilà** some sample
till tomorrow good-bye

conversations au téléphone. Write them in the blanks **en bas.**
on the

Je voudrais téléphoner au *(loo-vruh)* **Louvre.** _____

Je voudrais téléphoner à Chicago. *Je voudrais téléphoner à Chicago.*

Je voudrais téléphoner à Madame Le Gaul à Marseille. _____

Je voudrais téléphoner à Monsieur Le Gaul à Nice. _____

Je voudrais téléphoner à Air France à l'aéroport. _____

Je voudrais *(fare)* **faire un appel en** *(pay-say-vay)* **P.C.V.** _____
make collect call

Où est la cabine téléphonique? _____

Où est l'annuaire? _____

Mon numéro est 68-70-10. _____

(kel)
Quel est le numéro de votre téléphone? _____
what

Quel est le numéro de téléphone de l'hôtel? _____

Voilà une *(oh-truh)* **autre conversation** *(poh-see-bluh)* **possible.** Listen to **les mots et comment** they are used.
another

Thomas: **Allô, c'est Monsieur Cézanne à l'appareil. Je voudrais parler à**

Madame Villon.

Secrétaire: **Un instant, s'il vous plaît.** *(a(n)-stah(n))* **Ne quittez pas.** *(kee-tay)* **Excusez-moi, mais la**
one moment don't hang up but
ligne est occupée. *(leen-yuh)*
busy

Thomas: **Répétez ça, s'il vous plaît. Je parle seulement un peu de français.**

Parlez plus lentement. *(lah(n)t-mah(n))*
more slowly

Secrétaire: **Excusez-moi, mais la ligne est occupée.**

Thomas: **Oh. Merci.** *(oh)* **Au revoir.** *(ruh-vwahr)*

(ah(n)-kor)
Et encore une autre possibilité.
still

Christine: **Je voudrais des "renseignements" pour Angoulême, s'il vous plaît.**
information

Je voudrais le numéro de téléphone du Docteur Philippe Beauchamp,

s'il vous plaît.

Téléphoniste: **Le numéro est 86-45-06.**

Christine: **Répétez le numéro, s'il vous plaît.**

Téléphoniste: **Le numéro est 86-45-06.**

Christine: **Merci beaucoup. Au revoir.**

Téléphoniste: **À votre service. Au revoir.**
you are welcome

Vous êtes maintenant ready to use any **téléphone en France.** Just take it **lentement et**

speak clearly.

(noo-blee-ay) *(pah)*
N'oubliez pas that **vous pouvez** ask . . .
don't forget

Combien coûte un appel local? *Combien coûte un appel local?*

Combien coûte un appel interurbain pour Cannes? _____

Combien coûte un appel pour les États-Unis? *(lay)* *(zay-tah-zew-nee)* _____
to the United States

Combien coûte un appel pour Rome? _____

N'oubliez pas that **vous avez besoin de la monnaie ou d'un jeton pour le téléphone.**
need

87

Step 20

(may-tro-poh-lee-ta(n))
Le métropolitain, commonly called **"le métro,"** est le nom pour the subway. **Le métro à** *(may-tro)*

Paris est the quickest and cheapest form of **transport.** It is an extensive **système** which *(trah(n)-spor)* *(see-stem)*
transportation

has been expanded by an express line, **le RER (Réseau Express Régional),** going to *(air-uh-air)*

la banlieue de Paris. A Paris, et dans smaller **villes, il y a toujours l'autobus,** a slower *(bah(n)-lee-uh)* *(veel)* *(too-zhoor)*
suburbs   of   cities   always

but much more scenic means of **transport. Vous** may also wish to go by **taxi.** In that case, *(trah(n)-spor)* *(tahx-ee)*

trouvez a taxi station, hail a **taxi** on the street or have one called **à votre hôtel. Quels** *(tahx-ee)* *(kel)*
what

mots sont nécessaires pour voyager en métro, en autobus ou en taxi? Let's learn them *(nay-say-sair)*

by practicing them aloud **et puis** by writing them in the blanks **en bas.** *(pwee)*

(may-tro) **le métro**	*(tahx-ee)* **le taxi**	*(kahr)* **l'autobus/le car**

                  le taxi

(lah-ray)
l'arrêt = the stop _____

(leen-yuh)
la ligne = the line _____

(koh(n)-dewk-tur)
le conducteur = the driver *le conducteur* _____

(koh(n)-troh-lur)
le contrôleur = the ticket-collector _____

Let's also review **les verbes de transport** at this point.

(moh(n)-tay)
monter = to board/to get into_____

(day-sah(n)-druh)
descendre = to get off/to go down_____*descendre*_____

(shah(n)-zhay)
changer (d'autobus) = to transfer_____

(vwhy-ah-zhay)
88 **voyager** = to travel_____

Maps displaying the various **lignes** *(leen-yuh)* **et arrêts** *(ah-ray)* **sont généralement** posted outside every

entrée *(ah(n)-tray)* **de station** *(stah-see-oh(n))* **de métro.** Almost every **plan** *(plah(n))* **de Paris** also has a **métro** map included.
map of

Les lignes sont color-coded to facilitate reading. **Vous achetez les tickets** on entering **la**

station et vous pouvez acheter un ticket ou **un carnet** *(kar-nay)* **de dix tickets.** **Vous** must also
one book

decide if **vous** wish **première classe ou deuxième classe.** Check **le nom** of the last **station**

on the **ligne** which you should take **et** catch **le train** traveling in that **direction.** *(dee-rek-see-oh(n))* If **vous**

devez changer de train, look for **les correspondances** *(ko-ray-spoh(n)-dah(n)s)* clearly marked at each **station.** **Le**
must connections, transfers

système d'autobus works similarly. See **le plan** *(plah(n))* **en bas.**
map

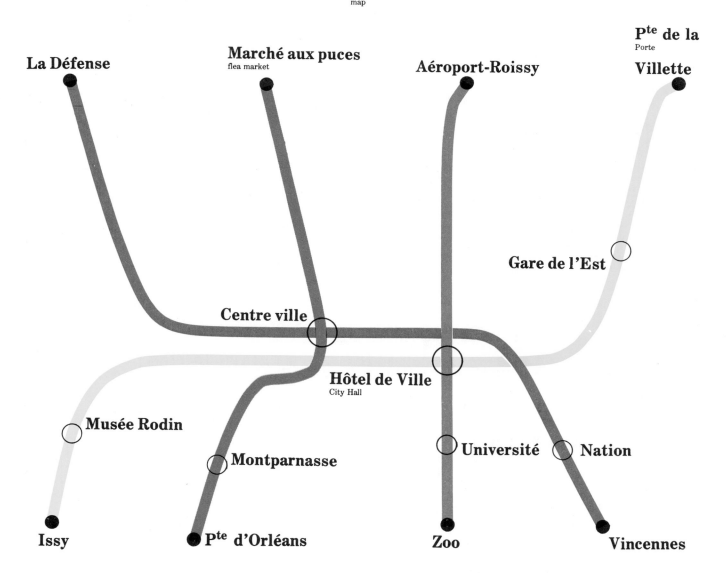

The same basic set of **mots et questions** will see you through traveling **en métro, en car,**
bus

en auto ou even **en train.**

Naturally, **la première question est "où."** *(pruh-mee-air)*

> Où est la station de métro? *(stah-see-oh(n)) (may-tro)*
>
> Où est l'arrêt d'autobus? *(lah-ray)*
>
> Où est la station de taxis?
>
> Où est la tête de taxis? *(tet)*
> head

Practice the following basic **questions** out loud **et puis** write them in the blanks **à droite.**

1. **Où est la station de métro?** _____

   Où est l'arrêt d'autobus? *Où est l'arrêt d'autobus?*

   Où est la station de taxis? _____

2. **Quelle est la fréquence des trains pour le Louvre?** _____ *(fray-kah(n)s) (day)*
   frequency

   Quelle est la fréquence des autobus pour Montparnasse? _____

   Quelle est la fréquence des taxis pour l'aéroport? _____

3. **Quand le train part-il?** _____ *(kah(n))*
   when

   Quand l'autobus part-il? _____

   Quand le taxi part-il? _____

4. **Quand le train pour Roissy part-il?** _____ *(rwah-see)*

   Quand l'autobus pour Roissy part-il? _____

   Quand le taxi pour Roissy part-il? _____

5. **Combien coûte un ticket de métro?** _____

   Combien coûte un ticket d'autobus? _____

   Le tarif c'est combien? *Le tarif c'est combien?*

   Combien est-ce que je vous dois? _____ *(dwah)*
   to you   owe

Maintenant that **vous avez** gotten into the swing of things, practice the following patterns

aloud, substituting **"autobus"** for **"métro" et** so on.

1. Où *(ess)* est-ce *(koh⁽ⁿ⁾)* qu'on achète *(nah-shet)* un ticket de métro? d'autobus? de train?

2. Quand part le train pour La Défense? pour le centre ville? pour Montparnasse? pour l'Hôtel de Ville? pour l'aéroport Roissy *(rwah-see)*? pour la gare? pour la Tour Eiffel?

3. Où est la station de métro pour aller à l'aéroport?
   to go

   Où est l'arrêt *(lah-ray)* d'autobus pour aller à la Tour *(toor)* Eiffel *(ay-fell)*?

   Où est la station de métro pour aller au *(oh)* centre *(sah⁽ⁿ⁾-truh)* ville *(veel)*?

   Où est l'arrêt d'autobus pour aller au Zoo *(zoh)*?

   Où est la station de métro pour aller au Musée *(mew-zay)* Rodin *(ro-da⁽ⁿ⁾)*?

   Où est l'arrêt d'autobus pour aller à la gare de l'Est *(lest)*?

   Où est la station de métro pour aller à l'université?

   Où est l'arrêt d'autobus pour aller au marché aux puces?

Lisez la conversation suivante, très typique *(tee-peek)*, et écrivez- la *(ay-kree-vay)* *(lah)* in the blanks à droite.
it

Quelle *(kel)* ligne va *(vah)* à Vincennes *(va⁽ⁿ⁾-sen)*? _____
which   *goes*

La ligne rouge va à Vincennes. _____

A quelle fréquence? _____

Toutes *(toot)* les dix minutes. *Toutes les dix minutes.*
every

Dois-je *(dwah-zh)* changer de train? _____
must   *I*

Oui, au centre ville. Vous avez une correspondance *(ko-ray-spoh⁽ⁿ⁾-dah⁽ⁿ⁾s)* à la station "Centre ville."
                              connection

Oui, au centre ville.

Il *(eel)* faut *(foh)* combien de temps d'ici à Vincennes? _____
it is necessary   *from here*

Il *(eel)* faut *(foh)* 20 minutes. _____

Combien coûte le ticket pour Vincennes? _____

Un franc cinquante. _____ 91

Pouvez-vous translate the following thoughts **en français? Les réponses sont en bas.**

1. Where is the subway stop? _____

2. What costs a ticket to City Hall? _____

3. How often do the buses go to the airport? _____

4. Where does one buy a subway ticket? _____

5. Where is the bus stop? *Où est l'arrêt d'autobus?*

6. I would like to get out. _____

7. Must I transfer? _____

8. Where must I transfer? _____

Voilà encore trois verbes.

(lah-vay)
laver = to wash

laver

(pear-druh)
perdre = to lose

(eel)(foh)
il faut = it is necessary

You know the basic "plug-in" formula, so translate the following thoughts **avec ces nouveaux verbes. Les réponses sont aussi en bas.**

1. I wash the jacket. _____

2. You lose the book. _____

3. It takes (is necessary) 20 minutes to go to Vincennes. _____

4. It takes three hours by car. _____

La Vente et l'Achat
(vah(n)t) selling   *(lah-shah)* buying

Shopping abroad **est** exciting. The simple everyday task of buying **un litre de lait ou une**

pomme *(pohm)* apple becomes a challenge that **vous** should **maintenant** be able to meet quickly **et** easily.

Of course, **vous** will purchase **des souvenirs** *(soo-vuh-neer)*, **des timbres-poste et des cartes postales,**

but **n'oubliez pas** those many other **choses** ranging from shoelaces to **aspirine** *(ah-spee-reen)* aspirin that **vous**

might need unexpectedly. **Savez-vous la différence entre une librairie** *(lee-brair-ree)* bookstore **et une**

boucherie? *(boo-shuh-ree)* butcher shop **Non.** Let's learn about the different **boutiques** *(boo-teek)* shops **et magasins** *(ma-gah-za(n))* stores **en France.**

En bas il y a un plan *(plah(n))* map **d'une section** *(sek-see-oh(n))* **de Paris.**

Sur les pages suivantes il y a all types of **magasins** *(ma-gah-za(n))* **en France.** Be sure to fill in the blanks

sous les images avec le nom du magasin.

(boo-lah(n)-zhuh-ree)
la boulangerie,
bakery
(oh(n)) (nah-shet)
où on achète le pain

(boo-shuh-ree)
la boucherie,
butcher shop
(vee-ah(n)nd)
où on achète la viande
meat

blah(n)-shee-suh-ree)
la blanchisserie,
laundry
(vet-mah(n))
où on lave les vêtements
washes   clothes

la boucherie

le café,
(bwah)
où on boit le café

(ka(n)-ky-yuh-ree)
la quincaillerie,
hardware store
(peel)
où on achète la pile
battery

(far-mah-see)
la pharmacie,
(lah-spee-reen)
où on achète l'aspirine

le café

(flur-east)
le fleuriste,
florist

où on achète les fleurs

(tah-bah)
le bureau de tabac,
tobacco store

où on achète le tabac
tobacco
(see-gah-ret)
et les cigarettes

(koh(n)-fee-suh-ree)
la confiserie,
confectionery
(boh(n)-boh(n))
où on achète les bonbons
(show-ko-lah)
et le chocolat

(lay-tuh-ree) (kray-muh-ree)
la laiterie/la crémerie,
dairy

où on achète le lait

(pah-tee-suh-ree)
la pâtisserie,
pastry shop

où on achète les pâtisseries
pastries

(mar-shah$^{(n)}$) (lay-geum)
le marchand de légumes,
seller   vegetables

où on achète les légumes

LA LAITERIE

LA PÂTISSERIE

LE MARCHAND DE LÉGUMES

(par-keeng)
le parking
parking lot

(gar)
où on gare l'auto
park

(kwah-fur)
le coiffeur,
hairdresser

(koop) (shuh-vuh)
où on coupe les cheveux
cuts   hair

(tie-yur)
le tailleur,
tailor

(vet-mah$^{(n)}$)
où on fait les vêtements
makes

LE PARKING

LE COIFFEUR

LE TAILLEUR

le tailleur

le bureau de poste,
post office

où on achète les timbres

(ko-mee-sah-ree-ah)
le commissariat de police,
police station

(poh-lease)
où on trouve la police

la banque,

(shah$^{(n)}$zh)
où on change l'argent et
exchanges
(toosh) (shek)
touche le chèque
cashes

LE BUREAU DE POSTE

LE COMMISSARIAT DE POLICE

LA BANQUE

(lay-pee-suh-ree)
l'épicerie,
grocery store

où on achète la viande,

les fruits et le lait

(shar-kew-tuh-ree)
la charcuterie,
delicatessen

où on achète le saucisson
salami/sausage
(soh-see-soh⁽ⁿ⁾)

(soh-sees)
et la saucisse

(fwee-tee-ay)
le fruitier,
fruit vendor

où on achète les fruits

L'ÉPICERIE

LA CHARCUTERIE

LE FRUITIER

(see-nay-mah)
le cinéma,

(vwah)
où on voit le film
sees

(kee-osk)
le kiosque,
newsstand

où on achète les

(zhoor-no)
journaux et les revues

(neh-twhy-yahzh) *(sek)*
le nettoyage à sec,
dry cleaning

où on lave les

(shee-meek-mah⁽ⁿ⁾)
vêtements chimiquement
chemically

LE CINÉMA

LE KIOSQUE

LE NETTOYAGE À SEC

le cinéma

(pah-peh-tuh-ree)
la papeterie,
stationery store

où on achète le papier,

le stylo et le crayon

(lee-brair-ree)
la librairie,
bookstore

où on achète et

(vah⁽ⁿ⁾)
vend les livres
sells

(grah⁽ⁿ⁾) *(ma-gah-za⁽ⁿ⁾)*
le grand magasin,
department store

(too)
où on achète tout
everything

(see Step 22)

LA PAPETERIE

LA LIBRAIRIE

LE GRAND MAGASIN

(mar-shay)
le marché, où on
market

achète les légumes et fruits

(sue-pear-mar-shay)
le supermarché,

où on achète tout
everything

(stah-see-oh(n))(day-sah(n)s)
la station d'essence,
gas station

où on achète l'essence

le supermarché

(lah-zhah(n)s) (vwhy-ahzh)
l'agence de voyage,
travel agency

où on achète les

billets d'avion

(lor-low-zhuh-ree)
l'horlogerie,
clock and watchmaker's shop

où on achète les horloges

(pwah-soh(n)-nuh-ree)
la poissonnerie
fish market

(pwah-soh(n))
où on achète le poisson
fish

Quand les magasins français sont-ils ouverts? *(oo-vair)* **Les magasins français sont généralement**
are they open

ouverts de lundi à samedi, de 9:00 à 18:30. **Beaucoup de petits magasins** will close over

the lunch hour **(12:00 — 14:00),** although this is increasingly less true **à Paris.** Some

foodshops **sont ouverts le dimanche, et** it is often a family ritual to make a trip **à la**
on Sundays

boulangerie où pâtisserie to pick up **le pain et** special weekend **gâteau.** *(gah-toe)* Many shops **sont**
cake

(toh-see) **aussi** closed **le lundi.** Local, open-air **marchés sont** truly **une expérience,** *(ek-spay-ree-ah(n)s)* so be sure to
also

check **les heures** *(lay) (zuhr)* of the one closest to **votre hôtel.**

(ee) (ah-teel)
Y a-t-il anything else which makes **les magasins français différents** from **les magasins**
is there

américains? Oui. Look at **les images à la prochaine page.** 97

3. *(twah-zee-em)* **(troisième)** *(ay-tahzh)* **Étage**

2. *(duh-zee-em)* **(deuxième) Etage**

1. *(pruh-mee-air)* **(premier) Etage**

(ray-duh-show-say) **Rez-de-chaussée**

En France the ground floor **s'appelle "le rez-de-chaussée."** *(ray-duh-show-say)* The first floor **est** the next floor up **et** so on. Now that **vous** know **les noms pour les magasins français,** let's practice shopping.

I. First step — Où?

Où est la laiterie?   **Où est la banque?**   **Où est le cinéma?**

Go through **les magasins** introduced in this Step **et** ask, **"Où"** avec **chaque magasin.** *(shahk)* each Another way of asking **où** is to ask

(ee)(ah-teel) *(pray)* *(dee-see)*
Y a-t-il une laiterie près d'ici?   **Y a-t-il une banque près d'ici?**
near   here

Go through **les magasins** again using **cette nouvelle question.**
this

II. Next step — tell them what **vous** are looking for, need **ou voudriez!**

1) **J'ai besoin de . . .** _J'ai besoin de_ _____

2) **Avez-vous . . . ?** _____

3) **Je voudrais . . .** _____

98

J'ai besoin d'un crayon.

Avez-vous un crayon?

Je voudrais un crayon.

J'ai besoin d'un kilo de pommes. *(pohm)*

Avez-vous un kilo de pommes?

Je voudrais un kilo de pommes.

Go through the glossary at the end of **ce livre et** select **vingt mots.** Drill the above patterns **avec ces vingt mots.** Don't cheat. Drill them **aujourd'hui. Maintenant,** take **encore vingt mots de votre** glossary **et** do the same.
more

III.   Next step — find out **combien ça coûte.**

1) **Combien est-ce?** *(ess)* _____

2) **Combien est-ce que ça coûte?** *(kuh) (sah)* _____

Combien coûte le crayon? *(koot)*

Combien coûte la carte-postale? *(koot)*

Combien coûte le timbre?

Combien coûte un kilo de pommes?

Combien coûte un kilo d'oranges?

Combien coûte un kilo de viande?

Using these same **mots** that **vous** selected **en haut,** drill **ces questions aussi.**

IV.   If **vous ne savez pas où trouver** something, **vous demandez** *(duh-mah$^{(n)}$-day)*
ask

Où est-ce qu'on achète de l'aspirine? *(lah-spee-reen)*   **Où est-ce qu'on achète des lunettes de soleil?** *(lew-net) (so-lay)*

Once **vous trouvez** what **vous** would like, **vous dites,**   **Je voudrais ça, s'il vous plaît.**

Ou, if **vous** would not like it,   **Je ne voudrais pas ça, merci.**

Vous êtes maintenant all set to shop for anything!

Step 22

(grah[n]*)* *(ma-gah-za*[n]*)*

Le Grand Magasin
department store

At this point, **vous** should just about be ready for **votre voyage en France. Vous** have gone shopping for those last-minute odds 'n ends. Most likely, the store directory at your local **grand magasin** did not look like the one **en bas. Vous** know already **beaucoup de mots et vous pouvez** guess at **beaucoup d'autres.** *(doh-truh)* / others. **Vous savez qu'** "enfant" est français *(know)* *(that)* pour "child," so if **vous avez besoin de** something **pour un enfant, vous** would probably look on the **deuxième ou troisième étage, n'est-ce pas?** *(duh-zee-em)* *(twah-zee-em)* *(ay-tahzh)*

6.ME ÉTAGE	boulangerie caféteria charcuterie alcool	volaille alimentation fruits légumes	produits congelés vin gibier viande
5.ME ÉTAGE	lits linge miroirs	ameublement lampes tapis	tableaux électroménager
4.ME ÉTAGE	vaisselle cristal	service de table ameublement de cuisine	clés faïence porcelaine
3.ME ÉTAGE	livres télévisions meubles d'enfant jouets	radios instruments de musique papeterie disques	tabac restaurant journaux revues
2.ME ÉTAGE	tout pour l'enfant vêtements de femme chapeaux de femme	vêtements d'homme chaussures d'enfant photo	toilettes antiquités
1.ER ÉTAGE	accessoires d'auto lingerie mouchoirs	maillots de bain chaussures de femme chaussures d'homme	équipement de sport outils mobilier de camping
R	parapluies cartes chapeaux d'homme bijouterie	gants maroquinerie chaussettes ceintures	pendules/montres parfumerie confiserie

Let's start a check **liste pour votre voyage.** Besides **vêtements, de quoi avez-vous** *(least)* *(vet-mah*[n]*)* *(kwah)* / what **besoin? Qu'est-ce qu'il faut en Europe?** *(kess)* *(keel)* / what / is necessary

(pass-por)
le passeport

(bee-yay)
le billet

(vah-leez)
la valise

                                      la valise ✓

(sahk)(ah)(ma$^{(n)}$)
le sac à main

(port-fuh-yuh)
le portefeuille

(lar-zhah$^{(n)}$)
l'argent

(lah-pah-ray)
l'appareil photo

(peh-lee-kewl)
la pellicule

(pruh-nay)
Prenez les huit labels **suivantes et** label **ces choses aujourd'hui.** Better yet, assemble
take

them **dans un coin de votre maison.**
         of

Voyagez-vous en France en été ou en hiver? N'oubliez pas. . .
                                     don't forget

(my-oh)   *(ba$^{(n)}$)*
les maillots de bain

(sah$^{(n)}$-dahl)
les sandales

(noh$^{(n)}$) (plew)
N'oubliez pas non plus the basic toiletries!
             either

(sah-voh$^{(n)}$)
le savon

                                      le savon ✓

(brohs)   *(ah)(dah$^{(n)}$)*
la brosse à dents

(dah$^{(n)}$-tee-frees)
le dentifrice

(rah-zwahr)
le rasoir

(day-oh-doh-rah$^{(n)}$)
le déodorant

(pen-yuh)
le peigne

For the rest of the **choses**, let's start **avec** the outside layers **et** work our way in.

(mah(n)-toe)
le manteau _____ ✓

(la(n)-pear-may-ah-bluh)
l'imperméable _____ ☐

(pah-rah-plew-ee)
le parapluie _____ ☐

(gah(n))
les gants _____ ☐

(shah-poh)
le chapeau _____ ☐

(boat)
la botte _____ _la botte_ _____ ☐

(show-sewr)
la chaussure _____ ☐

(show-set)
la chaussette _____ ✓

(bas)
les bas _____ ☐

(pruh-nay)
Prenez les quinze labels **suivantes et** label **ces choses.** Check **et** make sure that **elles sont**
take
(proh-pruh)   (rehst)
propres et ready **pour votre voyage.** Be sure to do the same **avec le reste des choses** that
clean   rest   of the

vous pack. Check them off on **cette liste** as **vous** organize them. From now on, **vous avez**

du "dentifrice" et non pas "toothpaste."
not

(pee-zhah-mah)
le pyjama _____ _le pyjama_ _____ ☐

(shuh-meez)   (nwee)
la chemise de nuit _____ ☐

(rohb)   (shah(n)-bruh)
la robe de chambre _____ ☐

(pah(n)-too-fluh)
les pantoufles _____ ☐

(puhv)   (plahzh)
La robe de chambre et les pantoufles peuvent aussi double **pour vous à la plage.**
can   beach

102

French	Pronunciation	English	Write	☐
le complet	(koh(n)-play)		_____	☐
la cravate	(krah-vaht)		_____	☐
le mouchoir	(moo-shwahr)		_____	☐
la chemise	(shuh-meez)		_____	☐
le veston	(veh-stoh(n))		_____	☐
le pantalon	(pah(n)-tah-loh(n))		_____	✓
la robe	(rohb)		_____	☐
la blouse	(blooz)		*la blouse*	☐
la jupe	(zhewp)		_____	☐
le chandail	(shah(n)-dye)		_____	☐
le soutien-gorge	(soo-tee-a(n)-gorzh)		_____	☐
la combinaison	(koh(n)-bee-nay-zoh(n))		_____	☐
les slips	(sleep)		_____	☐
le tricot de peau	(tree-ko) (poh)		_____	☐

Having assembled **ces choses, vous êtes préparé pour votre voyage.** However, being
(pray-pah-ray)
prepared

human means occasionally forgetting something. Look again at **le grand magasin**

directory.

À quel étage trouvez-vous . . .
on   which

vêtements d'homme?	Au ___2.me___ étage.
un chapeau pour une dame?	Au _____ étage.
livres?	Au _____ étage.
lingerie?	Au _____ étage.

cristal?   Au _____étage.

parfum?   Au _____.

vêtements de femme?   Au _____étage.

Maintenant, just remember your basic **questions. Répétez la conversation typique** *(tee-peek)* **en bas** out loud **et puis** by filling in the blanks.

Où est-ce qu'on trouve les pantalons de femme?_____

Dans le rayon de vêtements de femme. *(ray-oh^{(n)})* / department _____

Où est le rayon de vêtements de femme? _____

Au deuxième étage. *Au deuxième étage.*

Où est-ce qu'on trouve le savon et le dentifrice?_____

Au rez-de-chaussée._____

Aussi, n'oubliez pas de demander . . . *(duh-mah^{(n)}-day)* / ask

Où est l'ascenseur? *(lah-sah^{(n)}-sur)* / elevator _____

Où est l'escalier? *(leh-skah-lee-ay)* / steps _____

Où est l'escalier roulant? *(leh-skah-lee-ay) (roo-lah^{(n)})* / escalator _____

Whether **vous avez besoin d'un pantalon de femme ou d'une chemise d'homme, les mots nécessaires sont** the same.

Quelle taille? *(tie)*
size

_____

Quelle pointure? *(pwa(n)-tewr)*
size for shoes and gloves

_____

Ça me va. *(muh) (vah)*
me fits

Ça me va.

_____

Ça ne me va pas. *(nuh) (muh) (vah) (pah)*
doesn't fit

_____

Je prends ça. *(prah(n)) (sah)*
take that

_____

Combien est-ce?

_____

C'est tout, merci beaucoup.
that's all

_____

Clothing Sizes: **FEMMES**

chaussures									
American	5	5½	6	6½	7	7½	8	8½	9
Continental	35	35	36	37	38	38	38	39	40

vêtements					
American	8	10	12	14	16	18
Continental	36	38	40	42	44	46

blouses,chandails						
American	32	34	36	38	40	42	44
Continental	40	42	44	46	48	50	52

Clothing Sizes: **HOMMES**

chaussures									
American	7	7½	8	8½	9	9½	10	10½	11	11½
Continental	39	40	41	42	43	43	44	44	45	45

vêtements							
American	34	36	38	40	42	44	46	48
Continental	44	46	48	50	52	54	56	58

chemises							
American	14	14½	15	15½	16	16½	17	17½
Continental	36	37	38	39	40	41	42	43

Maintenant, vous êtes préparé *(pray-pah-ray)* **pour votre voyage. Vous savez tout** that you need.

The next step will give you a quick review of international road signs **et** then **vous** are off

to **l'aéroport. Bon voyage! Amusez-vous bien!**

Step 23

 = Dangerous Intersection

Voilà some of the most important **signalisations** *(seen-yal-ee-zah-see-oh(n))* **routières** *(roo-tee-air)* **internationales.** *(a(n)-tair-nah-see-oh(n)-nahl)* Remember
signs   road   international

that **en France** a basic rule of the road is **priorité** *(pree-oh-ree-tay)* **à droite.** **Conduisez** *(koh(n)-dwee-zay)* **prudemment!** *(prew-duh-mah(n))*
yield   to the right   drive   carefully

Bon voyage!

Danger

Dangerous
curve

Dangerous
intersection

Closed to
all vehicles

Prohibited for
motor vehicles

Prohibited for
motor vehicles
on Sundays and
holidays

No entry

Stop

Main road ahead,
yield the right
of way

You have the
right of way

Additional
sign indicating
the right of way

One-way street

Dead-end street

Detour

Traffic circle

No left turn

No U-turn

No parking

No parking or waiting

No passing

Speed limit

End of speed limit

Beginning of **autoroute**

Railroad crossing
240 meters

Railroad crossing
160 meters

Railroad crossing
80 meters

Customs

Federal Highway
Number

City limit

End of city limit

Parking permitted

Road ends, water
ahead

GLOSSARY

A

a/avoir .... has/to have
à .... at, to, in
  à côté de .... next to
  à demain .... till tomorrow
  à droite .... to the right
  à gauche .... to the left
accident, le .... accident
acheter .... to buy
addition, la .... bill in a restaurant
adresse, la .... address
aéroport, le .... airport
Afrique, la .... Africa
Afrique du sud, la .... South Africa
agence de location, la .. car rental agency
agence de voyage, la ..... travel agency
ai/avoir .... have/to have
aidez-moi .... help me! aid me!
AJ, la .... youth hostel
alcool, le .... alcohol
Allemagne, la .... Germany
Allemange de l'est, la .... East Germany
Allemagne d l'ouest, la .. West Germany
aller .... to go,one way
aller et retour .... round trip
américain (e) .... American
Amérique, la .... America
ameublement, le .... furnishings
amusez-vous .... amuse yourself
an, le .... year
ananas, le .... pineapple
anglais (e) .... English
Angleterre, la .... England
animal, le .... animal
année, la .... year
annuaire, le .... telephone book
août, le .... August
appareil, le .... gadget, appliance
appartement, le .... apartment
s'appeler .... to be called
appel de téléphone, le ..... telephone call
appétit, le .... appetite
apprendre .... to learn
approximativement ...... approximately
après-midi, le .... afternoon
arbre, le .... tree
argent, le .... money
armoire, la .... closet, wardrobe
arrêt, le .... stop, arrest
arrivée, la .... arrival
arriver .... to arrive
ascenseur, le .... elevator
assiette, la .... plate
assis (e) .... seated
attendre .... to wait for
atterrir .... to land
au .... in the, at the
auberge, la .... country inn
auberge de la jeunesse, la .. youth hostel
au coin .... on the corner
au milieu .... in the middle
au revoir .... goodbye
au-dessus de .... over
aujourd'hui .... today
aussi .... also
auto, la .... car
autobus, le .... bus
automobile à louer, la ..... rental car
automne, le .... Autumn
autoroute, la .... freeway
autre .... another
avec .... with
avez/avoir .... have/to have
avion, le .... airplane
avoir .... to have
avoir besoin de .... to need

B

avons/avoir .... have/to have
avril .... April

B

baigner .... to bathe
balcon, le .... balcony
balle, la .... ball
banane, la .... banana
banc, le .... bench
banlieue, la .... suburbs
banque, la .... bank
bas .... low
  en bas .... below, downstairs
basé .... based
bateau, le .... boat
beau .... beautiful
beaucoup .... many, a lot
belle .... beautiful
beurre, le .... butter
bicyclette, la .... bicycle
bien .... well
  pas bien .... not too well
bien sûr .... of course
bière, la .... beer
bijouterie, la .... jewelry
billet, le .... airplane/train ticket
billet de banque, le .... banknote
bistro, le .... restaurant
blanc, blanche .... white
blanchisserie, la .... laundry
bleu (e) .... blue
blouse, la .... blouse
boeuf, le .... beef
boire .... to drink
bois, les .... woods
boisson, la .... beverage
boîte aux lettres, la .... mailbox
bon/bonne .... good
bon appétit .... enjoy your meal
bonbon, le .... candy
bonjour ... good morning, good afternoon
bonne chance .... good luck
bonne nuit .... good night
bonsoir .... good evening
botte, la .... boot
boucherie, la .... butcher's shop
boulangerie, la .... bakery
bouteille, la .... bottle
boutique, la .... shop
brasserie, la .... beer-saloon, restaurant
bref .... brief, short
brosse à dents, la .... toothbrush
brouillard, le .... fog
bureau, le .... desk, office
bureau de change, le
.... money-exchange counter

C

ca .... that, it
cabine téléphonique, la . telephone booth
cabinets, les .... toilets
café, le .... cafe
café au lait ..... coffee and steamed milk
caisse, la .... cashier, register
calendrier, le .... calender
canapé, le .... sofa
car .... for
car, le .... bus
carte, la .... map
carte postale, la .... postcard
cathédrale, la .... cathedral
catholique .... Catholic
ce, cette .... that, this
ceinture, la .... belt
cendrier, le .... ashtray
cent .... one hundred
centime, le .... centime

C

centre, le .... center
cerise, la .... cherry
ces .... these, those
c'est .... it is
chaise, la .... chair
chambre, la .... room
chambre à coucher, la ...... bedroom
chandail, le .... sweater
changement, le .... change
changer (de train, d'autobus)
.... to transfer, exchange (money)
chapeau, le .... hat
charcuterie, la .... delicatessen
chat, le .... cat
château, le .... castle
chaud (e) .... hot
chaussette, la .... sock
chaussure, la .... shoe
chef, le .... cook
chemise, la .... shirt
  chemise de nuit, la .... nightshirt
chèque, le .... bank check
cher, chère .... expensive
cheveux, les .... hair
chien, le .... dog
cinquante .... fifty
clé, la .... key
coiffeur, le .... hairdresser
coin, le .... corner
colis, le .... package
combien .... how much
combinaison, la ..... slip (undergarment)
commander .... to order
commencer .... to begin
comment .... how
commissariat de police, le . police station
compagnie, la .... company
compartiment, le .... compartment
complet, le .... suit (clothes)
composer .... compose, dial (a telephone)
comprendre .... to understand
compris .... included
concierge, le/la .... doorkeeper
conducteur, le .... the driver
conduire .... to drive
confiserie, la .... confectionery
confiture, la .... jam
continuer .... to continue
contravention, la .... ticket
contrôleur, le .... ticket collector
corbeille à papier, la .... wastebasket
correspondences, les ...... connections
côté, le .... side
  à côté de .... beside, near, next to
couchette, la .... berth
couleur, la .... color
couloir, le .... hallway
couper .... to cut
courrier, le .... mail
court (e) .... short
cousin, le .... cousin (male)
cousine, la .... cousin (female)
coûte/coûter .... costs/to cost
couteau, le .... knife
coutume, la .... custom, habit
couverture, la .... blanket
cravate, la .... necktie
crayon, le .... pencil
crémerie, la .... dairy
cristal, le .... crystal
croissant, le .... crescent roll
cueillir .... to pick
cuiller, la .... spoon
cuisine, la .... kitchen
cuisinière, la .... stove
cuit (e) .... cooked
  cuit au four .... baked

D

dame, la .... lady
dans .... in
danse, la .... dance
de .... of, from
de, de l', de la, des, du .... some
décembre, le .... December
déclaration, la .... declaration
défense d'entrer .... do not enter
degré, le .... degree
déjà .... already
   déjà vu .... already seen
délicieux, délicieuse .... delicious
demain .... tomorrow
   à demain .... till tomorrow
demander .... ask, ask for
demi (e) .... half
départ, le .... departure
derrière .... behind
désir, le .... desire
deux .... two
devant .... in front of
d'ici .... from here
dictionnaire, le .... dictionary
difficile .... difficult
dimanche, le .... Sunday
dire .... to say
dit/dire .... says/to say
dix .... ten
dix-huit .... eighteen
dix-neuf .... nineteen
dix-sept .... seventeen
docteur, le .... doctor
donc .... therefore, so
dormir .... to sleep
douce .... fresh (water), sweet, soft
doucement .... softly, gently
douche, la .... shower
douze .... twelve
drap de bain, le .... bath sheet

E

eau, la .... water
école, la .... school
écrire .... to write
église, la .... church
elle .... it, she
elles .... they
en .... in
encore .... again, still
enfants, les .... children
entre .... between
entrée, la .... entry
   entrée interdite .... do not enter
   entrée latérale .... side entry
   entrée principale ..... main entry
entrées, les .... main dishes
entrer .... to go in, enter
envoyer .... to send
escalier, le .... stairs
escalier roulant, le .... escalator
Espagne, la .... Spain
essence, la .... gasoline
est, le .... east
est/être .... is/to be
est-ce .... is it
et .... and
étage, le .... floor, story
état, le .... state
   Etats-Unis d'Amérique, les ..... USA
était .... was
été, le .... summer
êtes/être .... are/to be
étranger, étrangère .... foreign
Europe, la .... Europe
européen, européenne ...... European
excusez-moi .... excuse me

F

exemple, le .... example
extrêmement .... extremely

F .... abbrev. for franc
facile .... easy
faim, la .... hunger
faire .... to do/make
faire un appel .... to telephone
famille, la .... family
farci (e) .... stuffed
femme, la .... woman
fenêtre, la .... window
fermé (e) .... closed
fête, la .... feast, festival
feuille, la .... sheet of paper
février, le .... February
fille, la .... girl, daughter
fils, le .... son
fin, la .... end
fleur, la .... flower
fleuriste, le .... florist
foi, la .... faith
football, le .... soccer
forêt, la .... forest
forme, la .... form, shape
formuler .... to formulate
fort (e) .... loudly
foyer, le .... hearth, lobby
frais .... fresh, cool
franc, le .... franc
français (e) .... French
Français, les .... the French people
France, la .... France
fréquence, la .... frequency
frère, le .... brother
frit (e) .... fried
froid (e) .... cold
fruit, le .... fruit
fumer .... to smoke

G

gant de toilette, le .... wash glove
garage, le .... garage
garçon, le .... boy, waiter
gare, la .... train station
gâteau, le .... cake
gauche .... left
   à gauche .... to the left
généralement .... generally
gibier, le .... wild game
glace, la .... mirror, ice, ice cream
gouvernement, le .... government
grand (e) .... large, tall
grand-mère, la .... grandmother
grand-père, le .... grandfather
grande serviette, la .... large towel
grands-parents, les ...... grandparents
grillé (e) .... grilled
gris (e) .... gray
gros, grosse .... thick, big
guichet, le .... counter, window

H

habiter .... to live, reside
haut (e) .... high
   en haut .... above
heure, la .... hour
hier .... yesterday
hiver, le .... winter
homme, le .... man
horaire, le .... timetable
horloge, la .... large clock
horlogerie, la
   .... clock and watchmaker's shop
hors-d'oeuvre, le .... appetizer
hôtel, le .... hotel
hôtelier, le .... hotelkeeper
huit .... eight

I

ici .... here
idée, la .... idea
identique .... identical
il .... it, he
île, la .... island
il faut .... it is necessary
il n'y a pas de quoi ....
..... you're welcome/it's nothing
ils .... they
image, la .... picture
imperméable, le .... raincoat
important (e) .... important
indicatif régional, le ...... area code
industrie, la .... industry
ingénieur, le .... engineer
institut, le .... institute
interdit (e) .... prohibited
intéressant (e) .... interesting
intérêt, le .... interest
intérieur, le .... inside, interior
   à l'intérieur .... within
introduire .... introduce, insert
Irelande, la .... Ireland
Italie, la .... Italy
italien, italienne ...... Italian

J

jambon, le .... ham
janvier, le .... January
Japon, le .... Japan
japonais (e) .... Japanese
jaquette, la .... woman's jacket
jardin, le .... garden
jaune .... yellow
je I
jeton, le ...... token for telephone calls
jeudi, le .... Thursday
jeunesse, la ...... young people, youth
jouet, le .... toy
jour, le .... day
journal, le .... newspaper
juif, juive .... Jewish
juillet, le .... July
juin, le .... June
jupe, la .... skirt
jus, le .... juice
   jus d'orange .... orange juice
juste .... just, fair, right

K

kilo, le .... kilo
kilomètre, le .... kilometer
kiosque, le .... newsstand

L

la, l', le, les .... the
lac, le .... lake
lait, le .... milk
laiterie, la .... dairy
lampe, la .... lamp
langage, le .... language
lavabo, le .... washbasin
laver .... to wash
leçon, la .... lesson
lecture, la .... reading
légume, le .... vegetable
lent (e) .... slow
lentement .... slowly
lettre, la .... letter
liberté, la .... liberty
librairie, la .... bookstore
libre .... free
lieu, le .... place
ligne, la .... line
limonade, la .... lemonade
linge, le .... linens
lingerie, la .... underclothing
lire .... to read

109

liste, la . . . . list
lit, le . . . . bed
   wagon-lit, le . . . . sleeping car
litre, le . . . . liter
living-room, le . . . . living room
livre, le . . . . book
local (e) . . . . local
   appel local, le . . . . local call
logement, le . . . . lodging
long, longue . . . . long
lorsque . . . . when
louer . . . . to rent
   voiture à louer, la . . . . rental car
lumière, la . . . . light
lundi, le . . . . Monday
lunettes, les . . . . spectacles

M

Madame . . . . Mrs.
Mademoiselle . . . . Miss
magasin, le . . . . store
   grand magasin, le . . department store
magazine, le . . . . magazine
magnifique . . . . magnificent
mai, le . . . . May
maillot de bain, le . . . . swimsuit
main, la . . . . hand
   sac à main, le . . . . handbag
maintenant . . . . now
mais . . . . but
maison, la . . . . house
majorité, la . . . . majority
mal . . . . poorly, badly
   pas mal . . . . not too bad
malade . . . . sick
manger . . . . to eat
manteau, le . . . . coat
marchand, le . . . . merchant
marché, le . . . . market
   bon marché . . . . . . cheap, inexpensive
   marché aux puces . . . . . . flea market
mardi, le . . . . Tuesday
marron . . . . brown
mars, le . . . . March
matin, le . . . . morning
mauvais (e) . . . . bad
menu, le . . . . menu
mer, la . . . . sea
Mer du nord, la . . . . The North Sea
merci . . . . thank you
mercredi, le . . . . Wednesday
mère, la . . . . mother
messieurs, les . . . . gentlemen
mètre, le . . . . meter
métro, métropolitan, le . . . . . . subway
meuble, le . . . . furniture
mieux . . . . better
mille . . . . one thousand
mince . . . . thin
minute, la . . . . minute
miroir, le . . . . mirror
mode, la . . . . fashion
   à la mode . . . . fashionable
moins . . . . less
   moins le quart . . . . a quarter to
mois, le . . . . the month
moment, le . . . . moment
monde, le . . . . world
   tout le monde . . . . everyone
monnaie, la . . . . coins, money
montagne, la . . . . mountain
monter . . . . to board/climb
montre, la . . . . watch
montrer . . . . to show
mot, le . . . . word
mousse, la . . . . whipped cream, froth
moutarde, la . . . . mustard
mouton . . . . mutton
multicolore . . . . multi-colored
mur, le . . . . wall

musée, le . . . . museum
muselman (e) . . . . Moslem
musique, la . . . . music

N

nation, la . . . . nation
nature, la . . . . nature
ne. . . .pas, n'. . . .pas . . . . . . no, not
   n'est-ce pas? . . . . isn't it?
nécessaire . . . . necessary
nécessité, la . . . . necessity
neige (il neige) . . . . it is snowing
neuf . . . . nine
neuf, neuve . . . . new
Noël . . . . Christmas
noir (e) . . . . black
nom, le . . . . name
nombre, le . . . . number
non . . . . no
nord, le . . . . north
normal (e) . . . . normal
Norvège, la . . . . Norway
note, la . . . . bill in hotel
nous . . . . we
nouveau, nouvelle . . . . new
novembre, le . . . . November
nuit, la . . . . night
numéro, le . . . . number

O

obligatoire . . . . compulsory
objet, le . . . . object
occupé (e) . . . . busy, occupied
odeur, la . . . . smell
oeuf, le . . . . egg
   oeuf mollet . . . . soft-boiled egg
   oeufs à la coque . . . . . . boiled eggs
   oeufs brouillés . . . . . . scrambled eggs
on . . . . one, people, they, we
   On fait ça . . . . one does that
   On dit que . . . . they say that
oncle, le . . . . uncle
ont/avoir . . . . have/to have
onze . . . . eleven
optimiste . . . . optimistic
orange, la . . . . orange
orchestre, le . . . . orchestra
ordinaire . . . . ordinary
oreiller, le . . . . pillow
organisé (e) . . . . organized
Orient, le . . . . Orient
où . . . . where
ou . . . . or
oublier . . . . to forget
ouest, le . . . . west
oui . . . . yes
outil, le . . . . tool, implement
ouvert (e) . . . . open
ouvrez/ouvrir . . . . open/to open

P

page, la . . . . page
paiement, le . . . . payment
pain, le . . . . bread
paire, la . . . . pair
pamplemousse, la . . . . grapefruit
pantalon, le . . . . pair of trousers
pantoufle, la . . . . slipper
papeterie, la . . . . stationer's
papier, le . . . . paper
papier-monnaie, le . . . . bills
paquet, le . . . . package
par . . . . by, per
par avion . . . . airmail
paragraphe, le . . . . paragraph
parapluie, le . . . . umbrella
parc, le . . . . park
pardon . . . . excuse me

parent, le . . . . parent, relative
parfait (e) . . . . perfect
   C'est parfait . . . . that's fine
parfumerie, la . . . . perfumery
parler . . . . to speak
partir . . . . to leave
pas bien . . . . not too well
pas mal . . . . not too bad
passe/passer . . . . . happens/to happen
passeport, le . . . . passport
pâtisserie, la . . . . pastry, pastry shop
pauvre . . . . poor
payer . . . . to pay
P.C.V . . . . collect call
peigne, le . . . . comb
pellicule, la . . . . film
pelouse, la . . . . grass
pendule, la . . . . clock
perdre . . . . to lose
père, le . . . . father
personnes, les . . . . people
petit déjeuner, le . . . . breakfast
petit (e) . . . . small
peu . . . . little
peuple, le . . . . people
pharmacie, la . . . . pharmacy
photo, la . . . . photo, photograph
   appareil photo, le . . . . camera
phrase, la . . . . sentence
pièce, la . . . . room, piece
pièce de monnaie, la . . . . coin
pied, le . . . . foot
pile, la . . . . battery
pilule, la . . . . pill
piscine, la . . . . pool
placard, le . . . . cupboard, closet
place, la . . . . seat, place
plafond, le . . . . ceiling
plage, la . . . . beach
plaisir, le . . . . pleasure
   avec plaisir . . . . with pleasure
plan, le . . . . map
pleut (il pleut) . . . . it is raining
plus . . . . more
pointure, la . . . . . . size (shoes and gloves)
poisson, le . . . . fish
poissonnerie, la . . . . fish market
poivre, le . . . . pepper
Pôle nord, le . . . . North Pole
Pôle sud, le . . . . South Pole
police, la . . . . police
politesse, la . . . . politeness
pomme, la . . . . apple
porc, le . . . . pork
porte, la . . . . door
portefeuille, le . . . . wallet
poste, la . . . . mail
   bureau de poste, le . . . . post office
   P et T . . . . post office
potage, le . . . . soup
pour . . . . for
pourboire, le . . . . tip
pourquoi . . . . why
pouvoir . . . . to be able to/can
pratique . . . . practical
premier, première . . . . first
préparer . . . . to prepare
préposition, la . . . . preposition
près d'ici . . . . near to here
printemps, le . . . . spring
prix, le . . . . price
problème, le . . . . problem
prochain (e) . . . . next
prolonger . . . . to lengthen
propre . . . . clean
protestant (e) . . . . Protestant
puis . . . . then
pull, le . . . . sweater
pyjama, le . . . . pajama

Q

quai, le .... platform
quand .... when
quarante .... forty
quart, le .... a quarter
   et quart .... a quarter past
   moins le quart .... a quarter to
quatorze .... fourteen
quatre .... four
quatre-vingt-dix .... ninety
quatre-vingts .... eighty
que, qu' .... what, that
qu'est-ce que c'est? .... what is it
quel, quelle .... which, what
Quelle heure est-il? ..... What time is it?
question, la .... question
qui .... who, what
quincaillerie, la .... hardware store
quinze .... fifteen

R

radio, la .... radio
rasoir, le .... razor
rapide .... fast
Rapide, le (RAP) .... train
rapidement .... quickly
rayon, le .... department
récepteur, le .... receiver
recette, la .... recipe, receipt
réciter .... to recite
reçu, le .... receipt
réfrigérateur, le .... refrigerator
religion, la .... religion
renseignements, les .... information
   bureau de renseignements, le ....
   .... information office
repas, le .... meal
répéter .... to repeat
répondre .... to reply, answer
réponse, la .... answer
rendez-vous, le .... appointment
réservation, la .... reservation
réserver .... to reserve/to book
restaurant, le .... restaurant
restaurant routier, le .... truck stop
reste, le .... rest, remaining
rester .... to remain, stay
retard, le .... delay
   en retard .... late
réveil, le .... alarm clock
revue, la .... magazine
rez-de-chaussée, le .... ground floor
riche .... rich
rideau, le .... curtain
rien (ne) .... nothing
robe, la .... dress
robe de chambre, la .... bathrobe
rose .... pink
rose, la .... rose
rôti (e) .... roasted
rouge .... red
route, la .... road
rue, la .... street
russe .... Russian

S

sac, le .... bag, sack
   sac à main, le .... handbag
saison, la .... season
salade, la .... salad
salle à manger, la .... dining room
salle d'attente, la ...... waiting room
salle de bain, la .... bathroom
salut .... hi
salutations, les .... greetings
samedi, le .... Saturday
sandale, la .... sandal
sang, le .... blood
santé, la .... healthy
saucisse, la .... sausage

saucisson, le .... salami, sausage
savoir .... to know a fact
savon, le .... soap
second (e) .... second
seize .... sixteen
sel, le .... salt
semaine, la .... week
sept .... seven
septembre, le .... September
serveur, le .... waiter
serveuse, la .... waitress
service, le .... service
serviette, la .... napkin, towel
   grande serviette, la ...... large towel
seulement .... only
signalisations, les .... signs
s'il vous plaît .... please
similarité, la .... similarity
simple .... simple, single, ordinary
six .... six
slip, le .... underpants
SNCF .... French national railroad
soeur, la .... sister
soir, le .... evening
soixante .... sixty
soixante-dix .... seventy
soleil, le .... sun
somme, la .... sum
sonnette, la .... doorbell
sont/être .... are/to be
sortie, la .... exit
   sortie de secours, la ... emergency exit
   sortie principale, la ...... main exit
sortir .... to go out
soulier, le .... shoe
soupe, la .... soup
sous .... under
sous-sol, le .... basement
soutien-gorge, le .... brassiere
souvenir, le .... souvenir
souvent .... often
spécialité de la maison, la ....
   .... specialty of the house
sport, le .... sport
standardiste, le .... the operator
station d'essence, la ...... gas station
stopper .... to stop
stylo, le .... pen
sucre, le .... sugar
sud, le .... South
Suède, la .... Sweden
suis/être .... am/to be
Suisse, la .... Switzerland
suivant (e) .... following
supérieur (e) .... superior, upper
supermarché, le .... supermarket
sur .... on
sympathique .... likeable, nice
système, le .... system

T

tabac, le .... tobacco
table, la .... table
tableau, le .... picture
taille, la .... size (clothing)
tailleur, le .... tailor
tante, la .... aunt
tapis, le .... carpet
tapisserie, la ...... tapestry, wallpaper
tarte, la .... pie
tarte aux pommes, la .... apple pie
taxe, la .... tax, charge
taxi, le .... taxi
télégramme, le .... telegram
téléphone, le .... telephone
téléphoner .... to telephone
téléphoniste, la .... operator
télévision, la .... television
température, la .... temperature
temps, le .... weather, time

terrasse, la .... terrace, sidewalk
tête, la .... head
thé, le .... tea
théâtre, le .... theater
thermomètre, le .... thermometer
ticket, le .... ticket
toilettes, les .... toilets
tour, la .... tower
tourner .... to turn
tout droit .... straight ahead
train, le .... train
transport, le .... transportation
treize .... thirteen
trente .... thirty
très .... very
trois .... three
troisième .... third
trouver .... to find
typique .... typical

U

un (e) .... a, one
unique .... sole, only, single

V

vacances, les .... vacation, holiday
vais/aller .... go/to go
vaisselle, la .... dishes
valise, la .... suitcase
vanille, la .... vanilla
variété, la .... variety
veau, le .... veal, calf
vendre .... to sell
venir .... to come
vent, le .... wind
vente, la .... sale
verbe, le .... verb
verre, le .... glass
vert (e) .... green
veston, le .... man's jacket
vêtement, le .... clothes
veuillez .... would you please
viande, la .... meat
vie, la .... life
vient/venir .... comes/to come
vierge, la .... virgin
vieux, vieille .... old
vigne, la .... grape vine
ville, la .... city
vin, le .... wine
vingt .... twenty
violet/violette .... violet
visite, la .... visit
vite .... fast
vocabulaire, le .... vocabulary
voie, la .... track
voilà .... there is/there are
voir .... to see
voiture, la .... car
   voiture à louer, la .... rental car
volaille, la .... poultry
votre .... your
voudrais .... would like
voudrions .... would like
vouloir .... to want
vous .... you
voyage, le .... trip, travel
   agence de voyage, la .... travel agency
   Bon voyage! .... have a good trip
voyageur, le .... traveler

W

wagon, le .... railroad car
wagon-lit, le .... sleeping car
wagon-restaurant, le .... dining car
W.C., le .... water closet, toilet

Y

y a-t-il .... are there/is there?

DRINKING GUIDE

This guide is intended to explain the sometimes overwhelming variety of beverages available to you while in France. It is by no means complete. Some of the experimenting has been left up to you, but this should get you started. The asterisks (*) indicate brand names.

BOISSONS CHAUDES (hot drinks)

café noir......................coffee, black
café au lait...................coffee with milk
café crème....................coffee with cream
café express..................expresso
café filtre....................filtered coffee
thé...........................tea
  au citron...................with lemon
  au lait.....................with milk
chocolat......................hot chocolate

BOISSONS FROIDES (cold drinks)

lait froid.....................cold milk
lait aromatisé.................flavored milk
eau minérale..................mineral water
  *Vittel
  *Perrier
  *Vichy
limonade ....lemonade
jus de fruits..................fruit juice
jus d'orange..................orange juice
jus de pomme.................apple juice
jus de tomate.................tomato juice
orange pressé................squeezed orange juice
citron pressé.................squeezed lemon juice
cidre........................cider
thé glacé....................iced tea
café glacé...................iced coffee

APÉRITIFS (aperitifs)   These may be enjoyed straight or over ice.

porto........................port
xérès........................sherry
Pineau de Charente..........grape juice and cognac
Kir ....Crème de Cassis and white wine
*Pernod/Pastis/Ricard........anise base
*Campari   *Martini blanc
*Cinzano   *Martini rouge
*Dubonnet   *St. Raphaël

COGNAC (cognac)   Cognac is a special type of brandy and is only produced in the region of Cognac.

*Rémy Martin   *St. Rémy
*Courvoisier   *Martell
*Hennessy   *Hine

CHAMPAGNE (champagne)   Champagne only comes from the region of Champagne.

*Dom Perignon (the monk who invented champagne)
*Mumms
*Piper-Heidsieck
*Taitinger
*Moët et Chandon
*Bollinger

LA GLACE.................ice

BIÈRES (beers)   There are a variety of brands including both **blonde** (light) and **brune** (dark). **La bière** is purchased in **bouteille** (bottle) or **à la pression** (draught).

PRESSION (draught)

*Kronenbourg Export
  le demi....................small glass
  le baron...................medium glass
  la chope...................tankard

BOUTEILLE (bottle)

*Kanterbrau
*Kronenbourg
*Pelforth brune
*Tuborg
*Paulaner

VINS (wines)   The wine production in France is closely controlled by the government, making it much easier to know what you are buying. You may drink wine by the **verre** (glass), the **carafe** (carafe) or the **bouteille** (bottle).

vin rouge....................red wine
vin blanc....................white wine
vin rosé.....................rosé wine
vin mousseux................sparkling wine

vin ordinaire................table wine
vin de table.................table wine
vin de la maison.............the "house" wine
vin du pays.................local wine of the region

A.O.C. (Appelation d'origine contrôlée)
  superior wine
V.D.Q.S. (Vins délimités de qualité supérieure)
  choice wine
Premier cru/Grand cru
  good vintage wine

The major wine-producing areas **de la France** are

Bordeaux   Bourgogne
Loire   Côtes du Rhône
Alsace   Champagne

ALCOOL (spirits)   Cocktail drinking is not wide-spread in France. The following are available in large, international hotels and **"Bars américains."**

gin ....gin
vodka ....vodka
rhum........................rum
whiskey......................scotch
bourbon......................bourbon
martini dry..................American martini

DIGESTIFS (liqueurs, brandies)

eau de vie...................grain natural spirits
fine à l'eau..................brandy and soda
*Drambuie   *Armagnac
*Cointreau   *Chartreuse
*Grand Marnier   *Bénédictine

La Carte

Préparation (preparation)

cuit	cooked
cru	raw
rôti	roasted
frit	fried
cuit au four	baked
grillé	grilled
farci/fourré	stuffed or filled
bouilli	boiled
fumé	smoked
mariné	marinated
braisé	braised
en croûte	cooked in crust
en cocotte	cooked in earthenware
au gratin	sprinkled with cheese
au lard	cooked in salt pork
au jus	cooked in its own juice
bleu	extremely rare
saignant	rare
à point	medium rare
bien cuit	well done

Autres (others)

French	English
confiture	jam
miel	honey
sel	salt
poivre	pepper
huile	oil
vinaigre	vinegar
moutarde	mustard
riz	rice
pain	bread
baguette	long loaf of bread
nouilles	noodles
pâtes	pasta
fromage	cheese
dessert	dessert
gâteau	cake
pâtisserie	pastry
glace	ice cream
chantilly	whipped cream
yaourt	yoghurt

FOLD HERE

Pommes de terre (potatoes)

French	English
croquettes	mashed, dipped and fried
gratin dauphinois	scalloped
frites	French fried
à l'anglaise	peeled and boiled
nature	plain boiled
maître d'hôtel	boiled and sautéed
purée	mashed
vapeur	steamed

Fruit (fruit)

French	English
pomme	apple
poire	pear
abricot	apricot
pêche	peach
banane	banana
orange	orange
mandarine	mandarin orange
cerise	cherry
prune	plum
pruneau	prune
melon	melon
pamplemousse	grapefruit
pastèque	watermelon
raisin	grape
raisin sec	raisin
grenade	pomegranate
ananas	pineapple
citron	lemon
compote de fruits	stewed fruits

Baies (berries)

fraise	strawberry
framboise	raspberry
mûre	blackberry
groseille à maquereau	gooseberry
groseille (rouge, blanche)	red or white currant
cassis	black currant
myrtille	bilberry
airelle	blueberry

Bon appétit!

FOLD HERE

Salades (salads)

French	English
laitue	lettuce salad
laitue chicorée	chicory
escarole	coarse-leafed green lettuce
endive belge	Belgian endive
mâche	wild field lettuce
romaine	romaine
mélangée	mixed
mimosa	green salad with egg yolks
mixte	mixed
niçoise	string beans, potatoes, tuna
verte	tossed green
de pissenlits	dandelion greens
de saison	seasonal
de tomates	tomato
vinaigrette	in vinegar and oil

Légumes (vegetables)

haricots verts	green string beans
haricots flageolets	small, pale green beans
petits pois	peas
lentilles	lentils
asperges	asparagus
carottes	carrots
épinards	spinach
poireaux	leeks
tomates	tomatoes
champignons	cultivated mushrooms
chanterelles	wild mushrooms
morilles	morel, wild mushrooms
chou	cabbage
chou-fleur	cauliflower
choux de Bruxelles	brussels sprouts
betteraves	beets
maïs	corn
concombres	cucumbers
navets	turnips
oignons	onions
radis	radishes
ail	garlic
artichauts	artichoke
aubergines	eggplant
courgettes	zucchini squash
macédoine des légumes	diced, cooked vegetables

Hors-d'oeuvres (hors d'oeuvres)

huîtres	oysters
assiette de charcuterie	assorted sausages, salamis
céleri-rave rémoulade	celery root in sauce
coeur de palmier	hearts of palm
crudités	raw vegetables
escargots	snails
foie gras truffé	goose liver with truffles
jambon cru	raw-cured ham
langue de boeuf gelée	beef tongue with aspic
pâté de campagne	country style, coarse pâté
salade panachée	mixed vegetable salad
saucisson	sausage/salami
terrine maison	house pâté in terrine
croque monsieur	grilled ham and cheese sandwich
croque madame	grilled chicken and cheese sandwich

Potages, soupes (soups)

bisque	cream soup with seafood
bouillabaisse	rich fish soup
crème de tomates	cream of tomato
petite marmite	soup-stew
pistou	vegetable soup
soupe du jour	soup of the day
soupe à l'oignon	onion soup
consommé	clarified stock
soupe à la reine	chicken soup with rice
velouté de légumes	thick vegetable soup
vichyssoise	potato and leek soup

Oeufs (eggs)

à la coque	soft-boiled
mollet	medium boiled
brouillés	scrambled
dur	hard-boiled
poché	poached
omelette nature	plain omelette
omelette au fromage	cheese omelette
quiche	cheese and egg pie
. . .à cheval	. . .topped with a fried egg
au plat	fried (sometimes baked)

Viande (meat)

Veau (veal)

blanquette de veau	veal stew with gravy
côte de veau	veal chop
côtelette de veau	veal chop
foie de veau	calf's liver
fricassée de veau	veal stew
jarret de veau	veal shank
médaillons de veau	discs of pan-fried veal
noisette de veau	tenderloin morsels of veal
poitrine de veau farcie	stuffed breast of veal
ris de veau	veal sweetbreads
rognons de veau	veal kidneys
rôti de veau	roast veal
tendron de veau	braised breast of veal
tête de veau	head of veal
escalope de veau	veal cutlet

Boeuf (beef)

boeuf bourguignon	red wine stew
carbonades de boeuf	sautéed and braised slices
côte de boeuf	beef rib steaks
daube de boeuf	marinated pot-roast
entrecôte de boeuf	boneless beef rib steak
estouffade de boeuf	braised beef in wine stew
filet de boeuf	tenderloin of beef
langue de boeuf	beef tongue
médaillon de boeuf	thick discs of tenderloin
queue de boeuf	oxtail
braisé de boeuf	beef stew in wine
tournedos	beef tenderloin
terrine de boeuf	casserole stew
tripes	stomach lining
moelle	beef bone marrow

Porc (pork)

côte/côtelette de porc	pork chop
carré de porc provençal	rib loin roast with spices
cuissot de porc	fresh ham roast
jarret de porc	pork shank
noisette de porc	small tenderloin discs
pied de porc	pig's foot
rognons de porc	pork kidneys
rôti de porc	pork roast
tête de porc roulée	rolled pig's head
cochon au lait	suckling pig (roasted)

Agneau (lamb)

carré d'agneau	lamb rib roast
côte/côtelette d'agneau	lamb chop
épaule d'agneau	lamb shoulder
gigot d'agneau	leg of lamb
cervelle d'agneau	lamb's brains

Viande (meat) continued

poulet	chicken
coq au vin	chicken in wine sauce
canard	duck
caneton	duckling
chapon	capon
caille	quail
oie	goose
faisan	pheasant
pigeon	pigeon
dinde	turkey

Volaille (poultry)

(see above)

Gibier (wild game)

gigue de chevreuil	roast leg of venison
bécasse	woodcock
escalope de sanglier	cutlets of wild boar
cuissot de marcassin	roast leg of wild pig
râble de lapin	saddle of rabbit
lapin sauté chasseur	rabbit sautéed in wine

Poissons et fruits de mer (fish and seafood)

anchois	anchovies
anguille	eel
cabillaud	codfish
calamar	squid
carpe	carp
colin	hake
coquillages	shellfish
coquilles Saint-Jacques	scallops
crabe	crab
crevettes	shrimps
écrevisses	fresh-water crayfish
flétan	halibut
grenouille	frog
hareng	herring
homard	true lobster, with claws
langouste	spiny lobster, no claws
langoustine	shellfish
morue	dried codfish
moules	mussels
oursins	sea urchins
perche	perch
poulpe	small octopus
quenelles	cylindrical fish dumpling
rouget de roche	Mediterranean red mullet
saumon	salmon
sole	sole
truite	trout
thon	tuna

(vuh-neer)
venir

(saw-puh-lay)
s'appeler

(ah-lay)
aller

(ah-shuh-tay)
acheter

(ah-vwahr)
avoir

(par-lay)
parler

(ah-prah$^{(n)}$-druh)
apprendre

(ah-bee-tay)
habiter

(zhuh)   *(voo-dray)*
je voudrais

(ko-mah$^{(n)}$-day)
commander

(ah-vwahr)   *(buh-zwa$^{(n)}$)*   *(duh)*
avoir besoin de

(reh-stay)
rester

to be called	to come
to buy	to go
to speak	to have
to live/reside	to learn
to order	I would like
to stay/remain	to need

(deer) **dire**	*(vah(n)-druh)* **vendre**
(mah(n)-zhay) **manger**	*(vwahr)* **voir**
(bwahr) **boire**	*(ah(n)-vwhy-ay)* **envoyer**
(ah-tah(n)-druh) **attendre**	*(door-meer)* **dormir**
(koh(n)-prah(n)-druh) **comprendre**	*(troo-vay)* **trouver**
(ray-pay-tay) **répéter**	*(fare)* **faire**

to sell	to say
to see	to eat
to send	to drink
to sleep	to wait
to find	to understand
to do/make	to repeat

(ay-kreer) écrire	*(leer)* lire
(moh(n)-tray) montrer	*(vwhy-ah-zhay)* voyager
(pay-yay) payer	*(trah-vhy-ay)* travailler
(poo-vwahr) pouvoir	*(prah(n)-druh)* *(lah-vee-oh(n))* prendre l'avion
(duh-vwahr) devoir	*(eel)* *(foh)* il faut
(sah-vwahr) savoir	*(fare)* *(vah-leez)* faire la valise

to read	to write
to travel	to show
to work	to pay
to fly	to be able to/can
it is necessary	to have to/must/owe
to pack	to know

(koh-mah(n)-say) **commencer**	*(prah(n)-druh)* **prendre**
(oov-rear) **ouvrir**	*(moh(n)-tay)* **monter**
(fare) *(kwee-zeen)* **faire la cuisine**	*(day-sah(n)-druh)* **descendre**
(ah-tair-ear) **atterrir**	*(day-bar-kay)* **débarquer**
(ray-zair-vay) **réserver**	*(shah(n)-zhay)* *(duh)* **changer de. . .**
(koo-tay) **coûter**	*(ah-ree-vay)* **arriver**

to take	to begin
to climb/board	to open
to go down/get out	to cook
to disembark	to land
to transfer	to book/reserve
to arrive	to cost

(par-teer) **partir**	*(fair-may)* **fermer**
(koh⁽ⁿ⁾-dweer) **conduire**	*(lah-vay)* **laver**
(few-may) **fumer**	*(shah⁽ⁿ⁾-zhay)* **changer**
(duh-mah⁽ⁿ⁾-day) **demander**	*(pair-druh)* **perdre**
(eel) *(nehzh)* **il neige**	*(zhuh)* *ᵗ(swee)* **je suis**
(eel) *(pluh)* **il pleut**	*(new)* *(sohm)* **nous sommes**

to close	to depart/leave
to wash	to drive
to exchange	to smoke
to lose	to ask
I am	it is snowing
we are	it is raining

(eel)
il
(ell)
elle } *(ay)* **est**

(oh) *(bah)*
haut - bas

(voo-zet)
vous êtes

(poh-vruh) *(reesh)*
pauvre - riche

(eel)
ils
(ell)
elles } *(soh⁽ⁿ⁾)* **sont**

(koor) *(loh⁽ⁿ⁾)*
court - long

(oh) *(ruh-vwahr)*
au revoir

(mah-lahd)
malade -
(ah⁽ⁿ⁾) *(bun)* *(form)*
en bonne forme

(eel-ee-ah)
il y a

(boh⁽ⁿ⁾) *(mar-shay)* *(share)*
bon marché - cher

(ko-mah⁽ⁿ⁾) *(tah-lay-voo)*
Comment allez-vous?

(vee-yuh) *(zhun)*
vieux - jeune

high - low	he she is
poor - rich	you are
short - long	they are
sick - healthy	good-bye
cheap - expensive	there is/there are
old - young	How are you?

(boh⁽ⁿ⁾) *(mow-vay)*
bon - mauvais

(veet) *(rah-peed)* *(lah⁽ⁿ⁾)*
vite/rapide - lent

(deuce-mah⁽ⁿ⁾) *(for)*
doucement - fort

(grow) *(ma⁽ⁿ⁾s)*
gros - mince

(grah⁽ⁿ⁾) *(puh-tee)*
grand - petit

(boh-koo) *(duh)* *(puh)* *(duh)*
beaucoup de - peu de

(show) *(fwah)*
chaud - froid

(oo-vair) *(fair-may)*
ouvert - fermé

(gohsh) *(dwah)*
gauche - droit

(doo) *(ay-gruh)*
doux - aigre

(ah⁽ⁿ⁾) *(oh)* *(ah⁽ⁿ⁾)* *(bah)*
en haut - en bas

(ek-skew-zay-mwah) *(par-doh⁽ⁿ⁾)*
excusez-moi/pardon

fast - slow

good - bad

thick - thin

soft - loud

much - little

large - small

open - closed

warm - cold

sweet - sour

left - right

excuse me

above - below